The Churches and the Kingdom

J. HAROLD STEPHENS

THE
CHURCHES
AND THE
KINGDOM

GREENWOOD PRESS, PUBLISHERS
WESTPORT, CONNECTICUT

Library of Congress Cataloging in Publication Data

Stephens, Julius Harold.
   The churches and the kingdom.

      Reprint of the ed. published by Broadman Press,
   Nashville.
         1. Kingdom of God--Biblical teaching. 2. Church--
   Biblical teaching. I. Title.
   [BT94.S78 1978]   231'.7   78-5676
   ISBN 0-313-20488-8

© 1959 · Broadman Press

Reprinted with the permission of the Sunday School Board
of the Southern Baptist Convention.

Reprinted in 1978 by Greenwood Press, Inc.,
51 Riverside Avenue, Westport, CT. 06880

Printed in the United States of America

10 9 8 7 6 5 4 3 2 1

Preface

THE WORD "church" is used in this book to refer to a Christian congregation. This local and visible organism is the thing designated by most occurrences of the word in the New Testament. It is generally recognized that a few occurrences cannot be understood as designating specific congregations. The meaning of the word in these instances is outside the problem that is studied here. Recognizing that "church" does not invariably refer to a local congregation in no way invalidates the present purpose to study the relationship of congregations to God's kingdom. Using "church" to designate the congregation is consistent with the ordinary New Testament usage.

The purpose of the writer is thus to deal with the differences between the churches and the kingdom in the present age. It is his desire to deal with them as current realities, with functions so related as to present the churches as the agents of the kingdom of God. Eschatological questions about the kingdom are, therefore, not discussed.

The main purpose of this undertaking is to endeavor to make a contribution toward correcting errors which grow out of false conceptions of the church and the kingdom, especially where there is an attempt to make the church and the kingdom identical.

The writer has been encouraged in the preparation of this manuscript by those who, along with the writer, have recognized a dearth of material on the subject in question. To be sure, much has been written on the subject of the kingdom, but there seems to be such a limited amount of writing on the general theme of the relationship of the church and the kingdom. A chapter now and then may be found; but Baptists may be called upon in the next few years to give more than passing attention to the subject.

The writer is indebted to Dr. W. R. White, president of Baylor University, for his very splendid treatment of the subject in a chapter of his book *Baptist Distinctives;* and to Dr. W. T. Rouse for the help received from the chapter "The Church and the Kingdom" in his book *The Kingdom of God.*

Other sources that have been very helpful are: *Our Doctrines* by Harold Tribble; *The Churches of the New Testament* by George W. McDaniel; *Worthy Is the Lamb* by Ray Summers; *Christ's Kingdom and Coming* by Jesse Wilson Hodges; *The Baptist Faith and Roman Catholicism* by Wendell H. Rone; *A Study of the Kingdom* by T. P. Stafford; *Evangelism, Christ's Imperative Commission* by Roland Q. Leavell. There have been many other sources, all of which it would be difficult to recall and to locate.

Above all, the writer has sought to rely heavily and constantly upon the Word of God, which is the only true authoritative source and to which we should all turn prayerfully, studiously, with open minds, responsive hearts, and submissive wills. The writer wishes also to acknowledge a debt of gratitude to Dr. Norman W. Cox for his patience and constructive criticism as he has reviewed the manuscript, chapter by chapter, during the time of its preparation. The writer is also indebted to Dr. Bob Ramsay for helpful suggestions in the preparation of the manuscript.

All Scripture references are from the King James Version unless otherwise stated.

Contents

One

The Root of Many Errors

I'VE BEEN INTENDING to join the church," was the disappointing reply of the lost man to the pastor after a compassionate appeal for him to repent of his sins and trust Christ as his personal Saviour. There are many people whose conception of salvation is so shallow that they never get beyond the idea that someone is only attempting to persuade them to unite with the church. There are many who have no other conception of becoming a Christian aside from just joining the church. They seem totally unaware of the need for, and meaning of, being born into the kingdom of God as a prerequisite to, and separate and apart from, church membership. It is often discouraging for the witness of Christ to explain at length the plan of salvation and have the unsaved person rebelling against what is being said with the thought of prejudice toward the church and church membership. It is likewise discouraging when the lost person seeks to salve his own conscience and presumes to please the soul-winner by a casual reference to a consideration of merely joining the church, when he first needs the Lord as his Saviour. There are people everywhere with whom we must deal and to whom we are responsible who think of getting into the kingdom of God, and finding security there, by just joining the church.

Surely, we need to face the errors that come from shallow and superficial conceptions of the church and the kingdom. Just as truth begets truth and love begets love, so does error beget error. One basic error may finally result in many errors. The writer has long been of the opinion that a number of false doctrines stem from an improper understanding of the churches and the kingdom. Many of the problems in the Christian world, resulting in so many controversies, have their origin along the lines mentioned. The writer does not claim to have searched out all of the errors pertaining to an unscriptural interpretation of the relationship, but there is an attempt to point out in this first chapter some of the more obvious errors that stem from beliefs and teachings that would make the churches and the kingdom identical.

One error with which we shall deal pertains to the failure on the part of many to comprehend the principle of one kingdom and many churches. There are those who insist upon making all churches one church or eliminating all but one church to correspond with the fact of one kingdom. To accomplish this, the Scriptures have to be perverted and the imagination has to be stretched.

The conception that the church and the kingdom are the same is so deeply imbedded in the thinking of some that they cannot visualize singularity pertaining to the kingdom and plurality pertaining to the churches.

Since there is one kingdom, and *if* there was only one church, and the two are supposed to be identical, then why did the Holy Spirit inspire the men of old to use two words with different meanings in referring to the two? Those who insist upon the church and the kingdom being the same lose the conception of any plurality of churches and always use the word "church" in a general, comprehensive, and universal sort of way. The term "church" as is most often used in the New Testament has to do with a particular church; and if many particular churches are involved, the plural designation "churches" is employed.

Paul addressed his epistle "unto the church of God which is at Corinth" (1 Cor. 1:2), or to one local or particular church. This same apostle had occasion to address an epistle to more than one particular church when he wrote the Galatians—". . . unto the churches of Galatia" (Gal. 1:2). It certainly would do violence to the Scriptures to substitute the word "kingdom" in either of these references, and yet this ought to be permissible if the terms are identical in meaning; and if so, they ought to be interchangeable in use.

An unscriptural ecclesiasticism which would swallow up all of the individual churches, and which destroys the very identity of the New Testament churches, is the result of conceiving of the church and the kingdom as one and the same; such a system completely destroys the autonomy of the local church.

Another error that stems from conceiving of the church and the kingdom of God as one and the same is the error of the doctrine of the universal church, which beclouds the important place of the particular, or local, church. The doctrine of a universal church will destroy the autonomy of each separate church or congregation, since one who thinks that he is a member of the church universal will naturally and logically feel that his loyalty belongs to the larger universal church. The universal church idea has led to having a man at its head called the pope, rather than Jesus Christ, and to an ecclesiastical organization which exercises power over the separate churches, for which we have no pattern in the New Testament. "The individual church may be defined as that smaller company of regenerate persons, who, in any given community, unite themselves voluntarily together, in accordance with Christ's laws, for the purpose of securing the complete establishment of his kingdom in themselves and in the world," wrote A. H. Strong.[1]

Since the definition of the church has been given, it is in order at this point to give a brief definition of the kingdom, which definition comes from *The Baptist Faith and Message*, approved by the Southern Baptist Convention in 1925, as follows:

---

[1] A. H. Strong, *Systematic Theology* (Philadelphia: Judson Press, 1907), p. 890.

The Kingdom of God is the reign of God in the heart and life of the individual in every human relationship, and in every form and institution of organized human society. The chief means for promoting the Kingdom of God on earth are preaching the gospel of Christ, and teaching the principles of righteousness contained therein. The Kingdom of God will be complete when every thought and will of man shall be brought into captivity to the will of Christ. And it is the duty of all Christ's people to pray and labor continually that his Kingdom may come and his will be done on earth as it is done in heaven.[2]

This also emphasizes the principle of the church as the agent of the kingdom. The Catholic definition of the universal church and the kingdom as identical places the authority of men where only the authority of God should be. From the Baltimore Catechism of Christian Doctrine we read the accepted definition of the Catholics for the church: "The church is the congregation of all baptized persons united in the same true faith, the same sacrifice, the same sacraments, under the authority of the Sovereign Pontiff, and the bishops in communion with him."

There is no scriptural authority for all churches being formed into one federation with a fallible human being at its head. It is a perilous thing to substitute the lordship of man for the lordship of Christ, which is the trend of those who make the kingdom and the church identical in interpretation and application. There is no place in the New Testament where all of the particular churches are considered as one with the conception of all meeting together in one place. It is the particular congregation that is emphasized in the assembly. The word *ekklēsia* can never be applied simply to all believers and denominations collectively. The particular churches will lose their sense of mission if they conceive of themselves as lost in the church universal.

The assembly of all believers in heaven will not come until after the local or particular churches have fulfilled their mission and until after the final advent of our Saviour.

Another error which stems from an improper relationship of

---

[2] *The Baptist Faith and Message* (Nashville: The Sunday School Board of the Southern Baptist Convention, 1925), p. 19.

the church and kingdom is from those who advance the idea of the invisible church. In the so-called invisible church Christianity and the application of the doctrines of the New Testament may become as invisible and as imaginary as the "church invisible." To profess a love for the invisible church may become a subterfuge and an escape mechanism for the love and loyalty that is due the visible church. Too often the love for, and loyalty toward, the invisible church never find expression in visible, tangible service.

The New Hampshire Confession of Faith, Article XIII, defines a church as a visible and local institution: "We believe that a visible church of Christ is a congregation of baptized believers, associated by covenant in the faith and fellowship of the gospel; observing the ordinances of Christ; governed by his laws; and exercising the gifts, rights, and privileges invested in them by his Word."

There is a sense in which the kingdom is invisible, but the churches as agents of the kingdom are quite visible. Evidences of the kingdom should be found in every church through the membership, mission, and message of the churches. The reference recorded in Acts 14:23-27 will clearly show that the church is a visible body: "And when they had ordained them elders in every church, . . . they commended them to the Lord, on whom they believed. . . . And when they were come [to Antioch], and had gathered the church together, they rehearsed all that God had done with them."

Any pastor may testify that it is much easier to preach to the visible church than to the invisible church. There is also much better fellowship in the visible church than in the invisible church.

The next error that we consider is that of confusing the assembled and the unassembled. To apply the term "the unassembled" to the assembled may create a real problem when one seeks to interpret the church and the kingdom as identical. To make the church and the kingdom identical in meaning will force an untenable definition and application of the word "church" as used in the English Bible. Most Bible students from the various denominations fairly well have agreed upon the meaning of the word "church," which is a translation of the Greek verb *ekkaleō*, which means "to call together, to convene." *Ek* means "out," which gives the meaning "called out" from the world. Historically, the word was used in reference to an organized assembly whose members were being called out from private homes or businesses to attend to public affairs. This meaning is in keeping with the self-governing Greek city-state of Acts 19:39, when the town clerk of Ephesus was trying to suppress the uproar over Paul's ministry and, in particular, to answer Demetrius and the craftsmen. He said, "But if ye enquire any thing concerning other matters, it shall be determined in a lawful assembly [*ekklēsia*]."

The organized assembly idea of the *ekklēsia* was used also in connection with the gathering together of national Israel in Old Testament times and was referred to in Acts 7:38: "This is he, that was in the church [*ekklēsia*] in the wilderness with the angel which spake to him in the mount Sina."

An overwhelming majority of the references in the New Testament to *ekklēsia*, or church, undoubtedly indicate a local assembly or congregation of the followers of Christ. If this be true, we cannot impose the meaning of "assembly" upon the scattered people of God over all of the world who are now in the kingdom of God and in whom now is the kingdom of God. There are millions of God's children throughout this world who never will be assembled together this side of their assembly in heaven around the King of kings and the Lord of lords, at which time there will be for the first time the general assembly of the saints. Certainly, a scattered, unaffiliated group of believers in Christ from China to Africa would not constitute an assembly and does not measure up to the requirements of an assembly. Therefore, the church and the kingdom cannot be thought of as synonymous or identical in meaning without being in obvious conflict with the accepted meaning and application of the *ekklēsia*.

The assembly, by the very nature of the word, requires a meeting place. This applies to the Greeks, Israelites, and Christians. The word is used a number of times in the Septuagint but never refers to an unassembled *ekklēsia*. While no one of these groups continued in session all of the time, they did meet at stated times for the transaction of business; and when they adjourned, the members expected to assemble again for similar purposes.

No one rightfully could be called a member of the assembly who never assembled; and yet there are people who may be in the kingdom of God who do not so much as claim affiliation with the assembly or the church.

The error of requiring church membership for salvation must be considered along with the other errors mentioned. This error also comes from interpreting the church and the kingdom as one and the same, and is related to the error of sacramentalism.

The error expresses itself in a dependence upon church membership for salvation. One might unite with every church of every denomination, be baptized in every one according to the various teachings on the subject of baptism, and still not be in the kingdom of God. On the other hand, if the church and the kingdom are the same, then one would get into the kingdom through uniting with the church. There is no place in all of the Word of God that teaches admittance or entrance into the kingdom of God through uniting with any church. Jesus said, "I am the door: by me if any man enter in, he shall be saved, and shall go in and out, and find pasture" (John 10:9). Since Jesus never taught church membership as the condition for salvation, he must herein have been declaring himself to be the door into the kingdom of God.

Religious bigotry has been bred in an atmosphere of making the church and the kingdom identical. There are two well-known groups—those who call themselves Catholics and those who call themselves the Churches of Christ—which strongly insist upon their particular church and the kingdom as being the same. If they sincerely believe this, it is quite easy to see how they would exercise judgment and pronounce doom upon all who are not members of their particular church. Their conclusion that all are lost who do not belong to their church to them is justified, since to be in their church is to be in the kingdom of God and to be out of their church is to be out of the kingdom of God. It is no problem for such people to express pharisaical pride and say to all of the rest of us, "You are on the way to hell because you do not belong to *my church*," which is *the* church, or which is the kingdom according to their teachings and beliefs.

Salvation must precede church membership, and church membership ought to succeed salvation. Every saved person should follow Christ in baptism and full church membership. It is not scriptural for a saved person to fail to so acknowledge, obey, and honor the Lord. Every child of God needs a church home in order to worship, serve, and grow in the Christian life. It is to be feared, however, that there are more unsaved people on all of the rolls of the churches than there are saved people who have affiliated themselves with no church at all.

There is no commandment for baptism that will ever apply to the impenitent or unbelieving sinners, and there is no place in the membership of any church for those who are not first of all born into the kingdom of God. "The kingdom is not to be identified either with a visible church or a visible denomination, but is the invisible and spiritual reign of God in the hearts and lives of believers, irrespective of denominational lines," according to E. Y. Mullins.[3]

Let us not overlook the error of the doctrine of baptismal regeneration, which is supported historically by the heresy that arose in the second century that baptism washed away all sin prior to baptism, and which is encouraged by the belief and teaching that the church and the kingdom are the same.

All major denominations of any description require baptism in some form and for some purpose before anyone is considered a full-fledged member of the church. Since this is true, to treat the kingdom and the church as the same thing will lead inevitably to the teaching of baptismal regeneration. It is obvious enough, and perhaps universally accepted, that no one can be saved now or

---

[3] E. Y. Mullins, H. W. Tribble, and W. O. Carver, *The Faith and Its Furtherance* (Nashville: Broadman Press, 1936), pp. 16–17.

ultimately without being in the kingdom of God. Salvation unto God is inconceivable outside of his kingdom. It is unthinkable that anyone will ever have a home in heaven who is not in the kingdom of God. The only logical and consistent conclusion at which the advocates of the oneness of the church and the kingdom may arrive is that the same requirements for church membership be likewise imposed upon kingdom membership. Then, if the two are the same, since water baptism in some form and for some purpose is the prerequisite for full church membership, baptism becomes the prerequisite for full kingdom membership.

This error has robbed Christ of glory in his being the only means unto salvation and casts reflection upon regeneration by the Holy Spirit, as requirements for salvation which are not found in the inspired Word of God are imposed.

An error that follows along closely with the error of baptismal regeneration and that stems from erroneously considering the church and the kingdom as identical is that of infant baptism. The line of false reasoning which accounts for the practice of infant baptism is somewhat as follows: If the church and the kingdom are one and the same and in order to get into the church one must be baptized, then baptism is essential to kingdom membership or salvation. Since we are conceived and born in sin, we are therefore sinners by nature. If we are sinners by nature, then the infants have that sinful nature. Something must be done to assure that the infants are in the kingdom, too. They must be baptized since, according to this false doctrine, baptism puts them in the church and the church is the kingdom.

In arriving at such extreme practices, another related error comes into being. It is the error of "religion by proxy." The infant is not old enough to make a decision and is incapable of asking for baptism or of knowing the *why* of baptism. The parents or guardian of the child must see to this; thus there is a religious rite being performed by others upon and for those who are incapable of making voluntary response, and this is supposedly "religion by proxy."

Another ramification of the errors associated with infant bap-

tism which may be traced back to the concept of oneness of the
church and kingdom is to be found in baptizing stillborn babies,
regardless of the extent of prematurity. This sort of thing is trace-
able to the reasoning that the soul is a reality from the time of
conception and is in no wise dependent upon the state of the
body.

The scriptural answer to all such religious absurdities and in-
congruities is to be found in the fact that God's Word places
clear emphasis upon the competency of each accountable being
in matters of religion and his relationship to God. The invitations
of God's Word are to the effect that to be accountable one must
be capable of making a choice, which involves personal ability to
reject or accept a person, a doctrine, an ordinance, or an invitation. This principle and privilege of choice was well stated by
Joshua when he said, "Choose you this day whom ye will serve"
(Josh. 24:15). It is also clearly set forth in the last great invitation of our Lord, who said, "Whosoever will, let him take the water
of life freely" (Rev. 22:17). The sin of wilful and deliberate unbelief and rejection of Christ is the sin for which the guilty person
is condemned. There is no condemnation for those who do not
reject Christ. An unaccountable infant is safe, under God's grace,
because such a one has not made a choice of Satan in preference
to Jesus. Jesus said, "He that believeth on him is not condemned:
but he that believeth not is condemned already, because he hath
not believed in the name of the only begotten Son of God" (John
3:18). The infant is incapable of believing or not believing; and
if condemnation comes from unbelief, the infant is not condemned.

The New Testament nowhere authorizes infant baptism. Jesus
never commanded that infants be baptized, and none of his early
disciples ever practiced infant baptism. John the Baptist, the
forerunner of Christ, never preached or practiced infant baptism.
It is an injustice to infants to baptize them, in that it may cause
them to rely upon this for their salvation after they have reached
the age of accountability. The church is to be composed of baptized, penitent believers in Jesus Christ; and infants cannot

qualify for this inasmuch as they are incompetent to repent of sins toward God and to trust in Jesus Christ. New Testament baptism is to be applied only to those who voluntarily submit to it, while the baptism of infants is imposed upon them. The commandment of Christ in the Great Commission is to baptize disciples, but no one can qualify as a disciple until he reaches the age of accountability.

The error of the church presuming to determine and control the subjects of the kingdom grows out of unscripturally relating the church and the kingdom. It is generally believed, whether practiced or not, that the churches have some disciplinary responsibility toward their membership. It is generally accepted that Jesus was dealing with the problem of disciplining church members when he gave his discourse that is recorded in Matthew 18:15-17. The conclusion of his instructions relative to the impenitent, non-co-operative offender was to ". . . let him be unto thee as an heathen man and a publican." Some think of this passage in terms of voting people out of the church, which would also presuppose the democratic procedure of voting people into the church.

The Roman Catholic Church, through the authority of the pope, exercises what is called the power of excommunication, that of putting an unruly member completely out of the church and withdrawing and withholding from him any and all privileges of church membership. This church also believes the church and the kingdom to be the same. The Churches of Christ (referring to the denomination by this name) also agree in a measure with the authority of the church in disciplining unruly members to the point of withdrawing from them so completely that they no longer have the privileges of church membership; this group also advocates the doctrine of the identity of the church and the kingdom. The error lies not in the exercising by the churches of the scriptural prerogative of disciplining wayward members but in the presumptuous claim that a church composed of fallible human beings could by any action remove anyone from the kingdom of God. For the sake of reasoning, if these people are correct in their claims for their church's being identical with the kingdom, then how presumptuous can they become in determining by human action whether a fellow being shall be in the kingdom or out of the kingdom? I am very grateful that no one human being and no group of human beings have been given the authority to determine my status in the kingdom of God or my possibilities of spending the future with my Lord in heaven.

The New Testament does teach, however, that the church has authority over receiving or rejecting those who are involved in the membership of the church. "Now we command you, brethren, in the name of our Lord Jesus Christ, that ye withdraw yourselves from every brother that walketh disorderly, and not after the tradition which he received of us" (2 Thess. 3:6). "Him that is weak in the faith receive ye, but not to doubtful disputations" (Rom. 14:1). These words of instruction are addressed to churches by the inspired apostle Paul; however, the churches do not by decrees or decisions determine the salvation of a soul but function in a democratic manner relative to membership and fellowship within a particular church that is an autonomous body.

A look at the church, the kingdom, and the state may help a person to discover other dangers that come from confusing the churches and the kingdom of God. The Roman Catholic Church also teaches the union of church and state. One error invariably leads to other errors and positions that are untenable and unscriptural. Jesus said, "My kingdom is not of this world" (John 18:36). And yet the union of the state and church reduces the kingdom of God to political levels when the church and kingdom are regarded as the same.

Jesus said, "Ye shall know the truth, and the truth shall make you free" (John 8:32). But in the union of church, kingdom, and state there is a strange mixture of authoritarianism which denies its subjects the liberty that God's children must have if they are the full recipients and beneficiaries of his truth. Under such a restricted system the victims have lost both liberty of conscience and freedom of worship.

The complete separation of church and state provides for the autonomy of New Testament churches. To a very real extent the ranking system of the various officials of the Roman Catholic Church and the over-all pattern of government have been patterned after the organization and government of the Roman Empire. Certainly, it was never intended that this kingdom of our Lord, which is not of this world, should ever be patterned after the order of pagan Rome, when one is our Master, even Jesus Christ our Lord. When there is an unscriptural union of church, kingdom, and state, the net result will be something that is quite foreign to the simple organization of the New Testament churches and to the spiritual and heavenly nature of the kingdom of God.

This kind of union of church, state, and kingdom leads to a substituting of the lordship of man for the lordship of Christ—a reducing of the spiritual to the level of the political and temporal and a creating of unholy and unscriptural alliances. In the pattern of the sovereignty of the "infallible" pope of Rome, the situation may become that of the pope and the Roman Catholic Church dictating the laws of both the kingdom of God and the kingdom of man. Concerning the separation of church and state, we quote here two paragraphs from W. T. Rouse:

In the divine economy, the church and the state are to function in separate and distinct spheres. The state is to concern itself with the temporal, civil, political, material interests of men. The church is to minister to men in the higher realm of the spiritual and eternal. Jesus never enunciated a principle calculated to help bring in His Kingdom more in keeping with His will, than when he set forth the principle of separation of church and state. "Render unto Caesar the things which are Caesar's and unto God the things which are God's" [Luke 20:25] is the divine plan. The state has no right to interfere with the church in its work of proclaiming the gospel; neither has the church any right to interfere with matters of state except as the individual members may by their individual efforts, through chosen political parties and otherwise, advocate purity of politics and righteous rule in the state.

Established churches, relying upon public taxation for support, are an abomination to God, standing where they ought not. God never intended that the state should rule over His churches. Union of church and state has been the occasion for untold tyranny and oppression, and has corrupted Christianity throughout much of the world. Wherever the principle of separation of church and state has been followed, peace, happiness, prosperity have resulted. Where the principle has been disregarded, injustice to men and harm to the cause of Christ have followed.[4]

In connection with this same line of thought we quote a pertinent paragraph by J. Wilson Hodges:

The basic question which confronts us is whether the kingdom which Jesus preached, and with which His gospel has to do, is a heavenly kingdom or potentially an earthly one; whether its working principles and its ultimate objectives are spiritual and universal, or are political and limited; in short, whether Christ's kingdom is wholly gracious and redemptive, or is in part, at least, legal and political. To the average Bible reader, the answer to this overall question is no doubt obvious enough—that is, that Christ's kingdom is definitely spiritual and redemptive both in its immediate and in its ultimate objectives.[5]

Any idea of a political kingdom on earth must not be confused with the true kingdom of God, which is a present reality but not without future glory.

---

[4] W. T. Rouse, *The Kingdom of God* (Dallas: Helms Printing Co., 1942), p. 189. Used by permission.

[5] Jesse Wilson Hodges, *Christ's Kingdom and Coming* (Grand Rapids: Wm. B. Eerdmans Publishing Co., 1957), pp. 21-22.

Two

Differences Between the Churches and the Kingdom

WHEN one thinks of the differences between the church and the kingdom, it must be remembered that the word "church" has been greatly abused. There are some groups and sects that are opposed in constitution, spirit, and purpose to all that the Word of God teaches about the churches that would apply to themselves the name "church." It is important to learn how to make distinctions. God's Word should always be read and studied with a discerning mind.

In pointing out the differences between the church and the kingdom, the simplest and perhaps the most obvious place to begin is in reference to the Greek word for church and the Greek word for kingdom. They are not the same words. Neither are the words synonymous in meaning.

The Greek word for church is *ekklēsia*. The meaning of this word when taken out of the setting of a New Testament church, and as it was used before the establishment of the church as we know it, should be considered.

B. H. Carroll defined the word *ekklēsia* as follows: "An organized assembly, whose members have been properly called out

15

from private homes or business to attend to public affairs." [1] The Greeks used the word *ekklēsia* to designate the legislative assembly at Athens—where the people were called from their homes to look after the public business and to participate in the plans and decisions to be made. J. H. Thayer gives essentially the same definition of *ekklēsia* as that of B. H. Carroll. The word was in use with well-understood significance long before the days of Christ in the world.

The called-out assembly idea of the word *ekklēsia* was to be easily applied to the New Testament church in apostolic times because of the historical meaning of the word. The Septuagint is a translation of the Old Testament Hebrew Scriptures into the Greek language under the direction of Ptolemy Philadelphus, king of Egypt during the third century before Christ. In the Septuagint the word *ekklēsia* is used more than one hundred times, and each time it has our English meaning of congregation or assembly. Therefore, when Jesus used the word *ekklēsia*, it already had the meaning of the called-out assembly in the minds of the people who heard him teach. This, of course, gives emphasis and impetus to the local or congregational concept of the church, which undoubtedly is intended much of the time that the word appears in the New Testament.

When there is an assembly of people in a given locality, the very nature of the case calls for the location of the assembly, which has given rise to the use of the expression "local" assembly or "local" church. In a sense, the meaning of the word *ekklēsia* makes the addition of the term "local" as superfluous as saying "tooth dentist." This meaning and application of *ekklēsia* was familiar to, and had significance with, the Greeks, the Israelites, and the early Christians; and in their assemblies they all had a similar understanding of its meaning for the present.

There is no place in the New Testament where all of the particular congregations are conceived of as being met together or

---

[1] B. H. Carroll, *Baptists and Their Doctrines* (Nashville: Broadman Press, 1913), p. 39.

all assembled at one place and at one time. Therefore, any universal assembly idea is ruled out.

There are, perhaps, a few references in the New Testament to the *ekklēsia* in an institutional sense. George W. McDaniel in his *The Churches of the New Testament* suggests that the word *ekklēsia* is used in its institutional sense fourteen times, and ninety-three times with the congregational or assembly meaning. But even as an institution the church must express itself tangibly and visibly in a particular congregation of baptized believers in Christ meeting in a particular place.

McDaniel's definition of the church is as follows: "A gospel church is an organized body of baptized believers equal in rank and privileges, administering its affairs under the headship of Christ, united in the belief of what He has taught, convenanting to do what He has commanded, and coöperating with other like bodies in Kingdom movements." It should also be pointed out in quoting McDaniel that he sees three references in the New Testament which refer to the church as the redeemed of all time assembled in glory.

There is not, and never has been, a functionally organized universal invisible church. Such an idea is not to be found anywhere in the New Testament.

The definition of a gospel church as given in *The Baptist Faith and Message* is as follows: "A church of Christ is a congregation of baptized believers, associated by covenant in the faith and fellowship of the gospel; observing the ordinances of Christ, governed by his laws, and exercising the gifts, rights, and privileges invested in them by his word, and seeking to extend the gospel to the ends of the earth. Its Scriptural officers are bishops, or elders, and deacons." [2]

In making distinctions between the church and the kingdom, such an appropriate definition of the church will enable the reader to make the distinction more clearly.

An entirely different word is used for kingdom. While the word

---

[2] *Op. cit.,* pp. 10–11.

ekklēsia in the Greek language is used for church, it is from the word *basileia* in the Greek that we have the English word "kingdom." It is appropriate, therefore, to make our first distinction between the church and the kingdom center in the difference in meaning and usage of these two important words. The word *basileia* denotes kingship, the possession of royal authority, reign, realm, kingdom, dominion, and subjects. Actually, a New Testament church does not even constitute the unit of the kingdom of God, to say nothing of a claim that would make the church identical with the kingdom. The unit of the kingdom is the redeemed, regenerated individual who has been born into the kingdom and family of God.

The reign of Christ the King is far more extensive and comprehensive than can be included in the meaning of *ekklēsia*. In the Gospels Jesus uses the word *basileia* [kingdom] more than one hundred times and the word *ekklēsia* [church] only three times. In the doctrinal epistles Paul uses the word *ekklēsia* thirty-eight times and the word *basileia* five times. The words "church" and "kingdom" do not coincide in meaning in any of these references or uses and by no means can become identical or interchangeable in meaning. The kingdom is not synonymous with the church, and it is not synonymous in meaning with any group of churches or denomination, but rather transcends all church and denominational lines. All of the redeemed of all ages—the young and the old, the rich and the poor, of every race and land on earth, or those now in heaven—belong to the family of God and are in the kingdom of God. "For this cause I bow my knees unto the Father of our Lord Jesus Christ, Of whom the whole family in heaven and earth is named" (Eph. 3:14–15). But only baptized believers are in the fellowship of a particular church or congregation, and even these entered the kingdom before they were baptized.

The bounds of the kingdom are far greater than the bounds of the church. His kingdom includes all who have repented of their sins toward God, have exercised saving faith in the Lord Jesus Christ, and have surrendered to Christ as the Lord and Master of their lives, thereby enthroning him in their hearts. His kingdom today upon this earth includes all who are redeemed from sin by the blood of Christ, who are saved unto righteousness and have been transplanted from the realm of darkness to light and delivered from the dominions of sin and Satan to the dominions of righteousness and Christ. His kingdom today includes all who, by the grace of God and in the power of his Spirit and under his direction, are seeking to do his blessed and holy will. His kingdom today includes all who are worshiping him in spirit and in truth and who are giving priority to his kingdom in their everyday lives.

The writer is of the opinion that the kingdom of God and the kingdom of heaven are used interchangeably in the New Testament and actually apply to the same thing in essence and meaning. It is reasonable, however, to assume that the expression "kingdom of God" may well place an emphasis upon God as the source and owner of his kingdom. Divine possession cannot be overlooked in any discussion of the kingdom. It is also reasonable to assume that the expression "kingdom of heaven" may be designed to emphasize the heavenly and spiritual nature of the kingdom in order to distinguish it from the perishable and corruptible kingdoms of this world. Jesus was careful to state, "My kingdom is not of this world" (John 18:36).

Matthew in his Gospel uses the expression "kingdom of heaven" about thirty times and uses "kingdom of God" less, but there is no reason to believe that he would make any real distinction between the two.

"The kingdom of heaven" must apply more to the quality of the kingdom than to the location, a concept which places more emphasis upon a present experience of salvation and a present relation to the kingdom with an assurance and a security rather than stressing some future entrance into the kingdom that is after death and that is problematical and speculative until it becomes a reality.

A quotation from Matthew 19:23–26 will indicate that Jesus used "kingdom of heaven" and "kingdom of God" interchangeably. "Then said Jesus unto his disciples, Verily I say unto you, That a rich man shall hardly enter into the kingdom of Heaven.

And again I say unto you, It is easier for a camel to go through the eye of a needle, than for a rich man to enter into the kingdom of God. When his disciples heard it, they were exceedingly amazed, saying, Who then can be saved? But Jesus beheld them, and said unto them, With men this is impossible; but with God all things are possible." Thus we also see that entrance to the kingdom of heaven, or the kingdom of God, is by being saved.

John A. Broadus gives the following definition of *basileia,* which is translated "kingdom":

The word *basileia,* which everywhere in English Version is rendered kingdom, means (1) "kingship," the possession of royal authority . . . (2) "reign," the exercise of royal power, or the period during which it is exercised; (3) "kingdom," the subjects, the organization, or the territory. In the sense of the territory it is not used in New Testament concerning Messiah's kingdom, and probably not in the sense of organization. Of the renderings kingship, reign, and kingdom, two would frequently be necessary, and sometimes all three at once, to express the full sense of the original term. As we have to choose one, the word "reign" is in this and many other passages a more nearly adequate rendering than "kingdom," and less likely to mislead.[3]

L. R. Scarborough gave this definition of the kingdom of God: "The kingdom of God is his reign in the hearts of men, through faith in the efficacy of the blood, and works of Jesus Christ."

W. O. Carver gave this definition of the kingdom of heaven: "The Kingdom of Heaven is both the reign of God and the realm in which that reign is operative. In its most intimate and actual expression, it is found in and consists of those persons who have by His grace voluntarily submitted themselves to, and committed themselves to, the will of God in Christ." [4] The simplest statement might be that the kingdom of God is that relationship between God and all of those who are his children and their relationships to one another under God.

---

[3] John A. Broadus, *Commentary on the Gospel of Matthew* ("An American Commentary on the New Testament," ed. Alvah Hovey [Philadelphia: American Baptist Publication Society, 1886]), I, 35.

[4] As quoted in Rouse, *op. cit.,* pp. 22–23.

A second approach in discerning between the churches and the kingdom is to point out certain distinctions that are involved in the differences in the very nature of the church and the nature of the kingdom of God. Reference here is primarily to that which is of this world and that which is not of this world. God's kingdom is one that is made up of "righteousness, and peace, and joy in the Holy Ghost" (Rom. 14:17).

Since the kingdom is of God and belongs to him, it must be spiritual, for "God is a Spirit" (John 4:24). The kingdom of God being spiritual, the weapons of the kingdom must also be spiritual rather than carnal and materialistic. Jesus never authorized and never used carnal weapons for his kingdom's work. He never intended that any external force should be used in defending or promoting his kingdom. While there are many carnal-minded people in all of the churches, the people of the kingdom are to be spiritual-minded. "That which is born of the flesh is flesh; and that which is born of the Spirit is spirit. Marvel not that I said unto thee, Ye must be born again" (John 3:6–7).

In further distinguishing between the nature of the church and the nature of the kingdom, an emphasis may be placed upon the fact that one is visible and the other is invisible.

The New Testament church is visible, audible, and tangible. Certainly, a congregation of baptized believers in Christ can be seen, felt, identified, heard, and located.

Scattered Israel in the land of Canaan is never called a church, because as such Israel was never assembled all together after the days in the wilderness and after the conquest of the Land of Promise. But the congregation in the wilderness is referred to as an *ekklēsia*, assembly, or church. Stephen made reference to "the church in the wilderness" (Acts 7:38).

A New Testament church not only has a visible membership and one that is clearly defined by name and number, but it is one that has a visible organization, with certain officers called for in the make-up of the church, such as pastors and deacons. A New Testament church has a visible meeting place, a regular meeting place that is definitely located. The place of assembly frequently was referred to in the Scriptures. Sometimes the meeting place was a home; consequently, we find such an expression as "the church that is in their house" (Rom. 16:5), which refers to the church which met in the house of Priscilla and Aquila.

While the church is visible, the kingdom of God is different in that it is invisible. Jesus says, "The kingdom of God cometh not with observation" (Luke 17:20). Not only does this statement distinguish the invisible kingdom from the visible church, but it also distinguishes the invisible spiritual kingdom from the kingdoms of the world which are territorial, political, temporal, and materialistic. If it is idolatry to make material images of God to worship, then it must be idolatry to make political and materialistic images within the kingdom, or of the kingdom, for worship. This would eliminate the idea of our Lord's reign as a political king over some material realm in the future.

As we pursue further the study of the differences relating to the nature of the church and of the kingdom, an emphasis should be placed upon the fact that the church is local and the kingdom is universal. This has been pointed out in other comparisons but must be linked with this series of distinctions.

The church as an assembly cannot congregate apart from that which has location. The *ekklēsia* is not something that is imaginary or abstract, but it is real. It involves a real place and has real business. The members of the church are given the invitation to assemble at a particular place, at a particular hour, on a particular day, and for a particular purpose.

The membership of a particular church is well defined by name and address. There is found in the New Testament a portion of the church roll at Antioch; it is given in Acts 13:1: "Now there were in the church that was at Antioch certain prophets and teachers; as Barnabas, and Simeon that was called Niger, and Lucius of Cyrene and Manaen, which had been brought up with Herod the tetrarch, and Saul." Now these on the church roll at Antioch were certainly not on the church roll at Jerusalem, and those listed on the church roll at Jerusalem were certainly not on the church roll at Antioch, but if they were all saved in both churches, they were in the same kingdom. While a church is local, the kingdom is universal in the sense that the kingdom incorporates in its membership and citizenship all of the redeemed of all of the world of all ages. God's kingdom is wherever there is a born-again person.

Another distinction in the nature of the church and the kingdom pertains to the difference in number. There are many churches, but there is only one kingdom of God.

The plural of church is frequently used in the Scriptures, but never the plural of kingdom. There were "the seven churches which are in Asia" (Rev. 1:4), "the churches of Galatia" (1 Cor. 16:1), and "the churches of Macedonia (2 Cor. 8:1); but the saved people in these various churches were in one kingdom, they had but one King, and they were under but one supreme authority.

The history of the church is different from the history of the kingdom of God. Of course, there has been a period since the establishment of the New Testament church in which the history of the church seemed more or less to determine and be parallel with the history of the kingdom. But the kingdom of God was a reality long before Jesus established the New Testament church; otherwise one would have to conclude that no one was saved until the church was established, which date of establishment some would insist was as late as the day of Pentecost but which must have been during the earthly ministry of our Lord. Much of the future history of the church and the kingdom may be similar, but this cannot be true of the past. The church was in its embryonic stages during the earthly ministry of our Lord, while the kingdom of God antedates this. Jesus took those prepared by his forerunner, John the Baptist, and used them as the nucleus of his new church. As time went on, Jesus gathered others for the early church as they were saved and baptized. They, too, along with the first ones, were taught, trained, organized, and assigned a task. Abraham, Isaac, and Jacob were in the kingdom of heaven centuries before this and shall continue to be in the kingdom. Jesus said "that many shall come from the east and west, and shall sit down with Abraham, and Isaac, and Jacob, in the kingdom of heaven" (Matt. 8:11).

The kingdom of God began on earth when the first true worshiper, Abel, brought an acceptable and excellent sacrifice unto God. The blood of the animal had been shed as atonement, in type, for sin. It was offered innocently and sacrificially and met the requirement of God, that "without shedding of blood is no remission" (Heb. 9:22). Abel was God's subject, the Lord God was his Master, and his sacrifice was pleasing unto God. There was even then a kingdom reality, a kingdom relationship, and a kingdom responsibility.

As in all of God's dealings with his people, his revelation has ever been on a progressive, ascending scale, until the kingdom of God today is more clearly defined and has more meaningful spiritual realities, more definite responsibilities, and higher standards than were ever known in Old Testament days. In some respects one might look upon God's dealings with his people in ancient times as merely revealing to them the kingdom in prospect, and yet there were many teachings of God for his people that were quite applicable to each generation, but with prophecies yet to be fulfilled for each generation. The kingdom of God today is still in progressive stages, even though it is also in the administrative stage and age.

There is hardly any way of determining the exact time and place for the establishment of the New Testament church in the ministry of our Lord. There was a process of organization and development which seemed to be rather gradual. It was certainly established during the days of our Lord's public ministry, which only lasted three and one-half years.

He referred to the church in Matthew 16:18, where he says that he will build his church. And he later refers to it as a functioning institution with responsibilities and ability to deal with differences between offending and offended members, and that in a disciplinary way, as is found in Matthew 18:17.

While the church was started somewhere around A.D. 26 or 27, the Scriptures make reference to the kingdom in this manner:

"Thy kingdom is an everlasting kingdom, and thy dominion endureth throughout all generations" (Psalm 145:13).

In the New Testament we find this word from the apostle Peter concerning those who were sure of their salvation, "For so an entrance shall be ministered unto you abundantly into the everlasting kingdom of our Lord and Saviour Jesus Christ" (2 Peter 1:11). While the kingdom is from of old in its history, yet this particular reference may be to some future aspect of the kingdom, with a present emphasis upon the everlasting nature of the kingdom. The kingdom was undoubtedly before the church. The early part of the four Gospels—including the annunciations, the ministry of John the Baptist, the Sermon on the Mount, and all of the parables—was devoted almost exclusively to the kingdom. The ministry of our Lord prior to that recorded in Matthew 16:18 dealt almost entirely with the kingdom of God rather than with the church as such.[5]

Another obvious and noteworthy difference between the church and the kingdom is in the terms upon which people are admitted to the church and those upon which they are admitted to the kingdom of God. For one to become a member of the New Testament church a personal acceptance of Christ as Saviour is called for, along with a public profession of faith in Christ, which is to be followed by church approval and church authorization for baptism by immersion. To get into the kingdom of God one must repent of his sins toward God, believe on the Lord Jesus Christ as his Saviour, and be born of God's Spirit into the kingdom and family of God. Baptism and church membership are not essentials or prerequisites for getting into the kingdom of God; and, unfortunately, many get into the churches without ever having been born into the kingdom of God.

Everyone who has been saved should be encouraged to be obedient in baptism and church membership, but Jesus never tied his own hands to his own organization, the church, so that he

---

[5] This analysis was made by B. H. Carroll, *The Four Gospels* ("An Interpretation of the English Bible," ed. J. B. Cranfill [Nashville: Broadman Press, 1913]), I, 154.

could not be the all-sufficient Saviour without membership in the organization, which he designed for the saved rather than for the purpose of salvation.

There is a further difference between the church and the kingdom, to be found among the members in their relationships. All who are in the kingdom of God are brothers and sisters in Christ, with family relations through having God as their Heavenly Father. Since not all who are in the church are in the kingdom, it becomes clear to us that not all church members are brothers and sisters in Christ, although all kingdom citizens are.

In considering the differences between those in the kingdom and those who are in the church, let us realize also that there is a vast difference in the security of those in the church and the security of those in the kingdom of God. The major groups which teach that the church and the kingdom are synonymous are the Catholics and the followers of Alexander Campbell. Both of these groups also teach that there is no security for their members who belong to the church-kingdom as they understand it. Their doctrine of insecurity for their members would indicate that one may fall out of the church-kingdom about as easily as he got in, entrance being by baptism. It seems strange and quite foreign to the Scriptures, and is a reflection upon the power of God and upon the security of his unshakable kingdom, that the subjects are able to get in and out so easily. How can there be such stability as the Scriptures teach concerning the kingdom that cannot be shaken and at the same time the instability of the constituents, who are in one day and out again the next, or in one moment and out again the next? The writer to the Hebrews emphasizes that we have received "a kingdom which cannot be moved" (Heb. 12:28).

There is such a strange and unscriptural mixture of the doctrines of the church and the kingdom by these people who make the two the same that the author has heard some testify that their salvation depended upon one church ordinance—their baptism. They lost it through failure to observe another ordinance—the Lord's Supper—and finally got back in the second time without baptism, which was the requirement for getting in the first time. What strange maneuvering of the church ordinances in this church-kingdom hybrid!

On this question of security, a saved man may withdraw from the church, but he will not and cannot withdraw from the kingdom. It is even possible for a saved man to be excluded from the church through severe discipline or to have the church withdraw fellowship from him, but it is not possible for one who is in the kingdom to be excluded from the kingdom, and the kingdom will not be withdrawn from any man who is born of God.

There is a commandment for the church to withdraw from the disorderly, but there is no authority to put anyone out of the kingdom of God. Paul wrote, "Now we command you, brethren, in the name of our Lord Jesus Christ, that ye withdraw yourselves from every brother that walketh disorderly, and not after the tradition which he received of us" (2 Thess. 3:6). A person's standing in the church may be lost, but his standing in the kingdom is secure.

When the church and the kingdom of God are compared and contrasted, a difference in the organization and government of the two may be seen. The churches have elected and ordained officers, which are not found in the kingdom as such. Every well-organized New Testament church has two types of ordained officers, namely, the pastor and the deacons, so that it is more than a conglomerate congregation. The officers of a New Testament church have certain well-defined duties. The duties are so assigned as to permit the pastors to devote much of their time to prayer, the study of the Word of God, and the preaching of the gospel. Varying ranks among church officers should have no place in the church. Every officer and every member should be looked upon as servants of the Lord through the church.

The *ekklēsia* is not simply the assembly of a group of unrelated people. It is the assembly of a group of people blessed with certain qualifications, requirements, and responsibilities in the way of regeneration, baptism, worship, and service. Beyond these initial requirements the *ekklēsia* is still more than a mere assembly of those thus qualified. It is the assembly of an organized group. The New Testament church is both an organism and an organization.

The kingdom of God has no organization, as we term it. The supreme ruler is Christ the King, and we are his subjects. Beyond him there is no authority.

The church is organized and authorized to be the custodian of certain ordinances. The church has two ordinances: that of baptism, which may be considered the initial rite into church membership, and the recurring ordinance of the Lord's Supper.

These are not kingdom ordinances but church ordinances. It is not necessary to observe either of them in order to get into the kingdom of God or in order to stay in the kingdom of God. They are not Christian ordinances in the sense of isolating them from the church, but they are church ordinances for Christians who are willing and qualified to meet the conditions of church membership.

The kingdom of God in comparison with the government of the New Testament church is not a democracy, but is rather a theocracy, where there is the direct and personal rule of the Lord Jesus Christ as the King, into whose hands all power has been committed by the Heavenly Father. His followers and his constituents did not elect him to his office as King, but rather he was born as the King. Jesus, in answering some questions of Pilate relative to his kingship, said, "To this end was I born, and for this cause came I into the world, that I should bear witness unto the truth" (John 18:37). In substance he is saying, "I was born to be the king of truth." While Jesus is the absolute King in his kingdom, many have vainly aspired to get in where the "kingin' was done," and have in attitude, word, and action pushed Jesus aside, substituting themselves and their own petty schemes for the lordship of the Son of God, our eternal King.

The laws of his kingdom are not to be changed. They need no revision. They are always up-to-date because they have eternal merit, and there is no authority on earth that can change the laws of his kingdom.

The kingdom of God is a theocracy, while the New Testament churches are to be democracies. As democratic bodies no church has any authority over another church. No group of churches, not even all of the churches combined, can exercise authority over one church; any such jurisdiction from one or by many churches over another church is contrary to New Testament teachings. This does not mean, however, that fellowship may not be withdrawn from any church or churches that seem to be conducting their affairs in conflict with the principles of the New Testament. Autonomy does not preclude voluntary co-operation and does not bestow upon any church the right to deny the faith.

The particular congregation is to have charge of its own affairs. There was never any hierarchy found among the apostles or in the early New Testament churches. Each separate congregation of baptized believers in Christ is an autonomous body.

In the New Testament churches the method of government is democratic. Everybody is somebody in a New Testament church, from the poorest to the richest, from the youngest to the oldest, from the least to the greatest, from the unlearned to the most learned. There is an equality among the members as to rank and privileges of discussing, commenting, and voting upon issues before the body. The New Testament church ought to be the purest democracy on earth as it functions in calling a pastor, electing other officers, and in the transaction of business.

The policies, meetings, schedules, and bylaws of a church may be subject to constant changes, according to the desires of the members who make up the spiritual democracy and according to the growing needs of a growing church in a changing world; but no church has any right to tamper with the laws of God's kingdom or to add to, or take anything from, the Word of God.

In the light of all of these obvious and scriptural differences between the church and the kingdom, one may be made to wonder how anyone can consider them as being identical or synonymous in meaning.

Three

Similarities Between the Churches and the Kingdom

WHILE emphasis has been given to the *differences* between the church and the kingdom, at the same time an unbiased study of the subject before us calls for a consideration of some of the *similarities* between the churches and the kingdom of God.

The logical starting place for pointing out similarities has to do with divine ownership and authority. Our Lord is pleased to claim both the church and the kingdom as his own, inasmuch as he uses the possessive pronoun in referring to each one. With reference to the church he said, "I will build my church" (Matt. 16:18). It seems that such an emphasis on his ownership of the church should clarify any confused thoughts that might have cluttered up the minds of the people concerning the Greek and the Hebrew assemblies. For his followers this is a new and unique sort of *ekklēsia* belonging to the Lord.

While Jesus is pleased to say "my church," he is also pleased to say "my kingdom." He said, "My kingdom is not of this world" (John 18:36). In this reference to the divine ownership of the kingdom, he is setting his kingdom apart from all kingdoms that have ever been in this world.

The same authority that established the kingdom has also established the churches, and we must conclude that both are of divine origin. The government of his kingdom rests upon him, as we are taught even in the prophecy of the coming Messiah and King. "For unto us a child is born, unto us a son is given: and the government shall be upon his shoulder: and his name shall be called Wonderful, Counsellor, The mighty God, The everlasting Father, The Prince of Peace" (Isa. 9:6).

This reign of our Lord is prophesied as a continuing and expanding reign and one that is ordered and authorized by him. "Of the increase of his government and peace there shall be no end, upon the throne of David, and upon his kingdom, to order it, and to establish it with judgment and with justice from henceforth even for ever. The zeal of the Lord of hosts will perform this" (Isa. 9:7). The reference to the throne of David must be figurative language, because David's kingdom was of this world —political, materialistic, and temporal. Jesus' kingdom is not of this world; it is spiritual and eternal and cannot be reduced to the level of the carnal, the temporal, the political, and the material.

The apostle Paul makes some very comprehensive statements in his letter to the Colossians about the creative, authoritative, and administrative work of our Lord: "For by him were all things created, that are in heaven, and that are in earth, visible and invisible, whether they be thrones, or dominions, or principalities, or powers: all things were created by him, and for him: And he is before all things, and by him all things consist. And he is the head of the body, the church: who is the beginning, the firstborn from the dead; that in all things he might have the preeminence" (Col. 1:16–18). The sovereignty of our Lord is to be recognized and honored both in his churches and in his kingdom. He is in supreme command in each, and his lordship is to be unquestioned.

As the divine owner of his kingdom and his churches, it is his prerogative to design all of the plans for each, to issue all of the orders for each, to reveal all of his purposes for each, to execute all of his will for each, and to give all of his instructions to each. As the owner and head of both the churches and the kingdom, he always gives orders that harmonize for eternal purposes, that are for God's glory and for the good of his subjects. It is inconceivable that he, as the owner and head of both, would ever issue any conflicting orders for his church or his kingdom.

As the divine owner and as the divine authority in the churches and the kingdom, for "the Father . . . hath committed all judgment unto the Son" (John 5:22), his presence is in and with both the church and the kingdom. While he occupies the throne of his kingdom, he has at the same time assured his churches of his accompanying presence as the churches obediently carry out his commission. "And, lo, I am with you alway, even unto the end of the world" (Matt. 28:20).

His pre-eminence in the visible church emphasizes, illustrates, and promotes his pre-eminence in every area of the kingdom and in all of life. "He is the head of the body, the church: . . . that in all things he might have the preeminence" (Col. 1:18). "For the husband is the head of the wife, even as Christ is the head of the church: and he is the saviour of the body" (Eph. 5:23).

The saved people in the churches and those who are in the kingdom belong to God. God has much to say in the Scriptures about the ownership of his people. Even when his people are wayward and negligent, he still calls them "my people," as in 2 Chronicles 7:14 when he calls upon his people to repent. The apostle Paul quotes some Old Testament passage in writing to a New Testament church: "Ye are the temple of the living God; as God hath said, I will dwell in them, and walk in them; and I will be their God, and they shall be my people" (2 Cor. 6:16).

Another similarity between the churches and the kingdom of God is in the fact that the individual is the unit in both the churches and the kingdom.

Baptists have always stressed the cardinal doctrine of the worth and competency of the individual. Every accountable individual must have the privilege, and certainly does have the responsibility and the ability, personally to turn from sin to trust the Saviour,

without the aid of parent, priest, or proxy in the sense of someone else's taking over the privileges and responsibilities of the individual. Every accountable individual is privileged to approach
God directly through Jesus Christ as the all-sufficient high priest.

The dignity and worth of the individual must not be en-
croached upon by contracts or commitments which rob unborn
children of the God-given right personally to choose the Lord,
personally to choose his church, and consciously to obey him in
baptism.

The competency of the individual is further to be recognized in
making the Bible an open book in his hands, with the personal
privilege of reading it, interpreting it, and applying it as the Holy
Spirit shall lead this individual. The individual, as the unit in the
churches as well as in the kingdom, further illustrates the responsibility for personal service in the kingdom through the church.
There is a place of service for everyone in the kingdom through
the church; and God is not pleased when an individual hides in
the crowd or is being swallowed by the crowd. Everyone is precious in God's sight, and the masses are never so great as to hide
the individual from the all-seeing eye of God. God deals with us
all as individuals. He is the God of the masses—as "the Lord God
of hosts"—but he is also the God of the individual—as "the God
of Abraham, of Isaac, and Jacob."

It is a sin against God as well as against the dignity and worth
of the individual when ecclesiastical systems that exalt a few tend
to lose sight of the individual so precious before God. The individual must have the right to worship God according to the dictates of his own conscience and must not be coerced in any sense
in his relationship to God, his kingdom, and his church.

Not only is a similarity between the church and the kingdom to
be found in the fact that the redeemed individual is the unit in
both the church and the kingdom, but also the individuals in both
the church and the kingdom are to enjoy a position of equality in
each one and before God, regardless of who they are, inasmuch
as "God is no respecter of persons" (Acts 10:34). Both the church
and the kingdom are made up of equals before God. All of God's

children are equally loved by the same Heavenly Father, and they are all brothers and sisters in Christ, having been redeemed by the same Saviour. Likewise, there is no place in a New Testament church for any kind of a ranking system, where one member must bow before another or be the servant of the other, outside of a mutual relationship of love in Christian service.

All who are in the kingdom of God have equal access to the throne of grace in prayer, and all may enjoy an equal security. Likewise, every member of the church has equal access to the privileges and blessings of church membership. All of those in the kingdom must lose sight of selfish interests in expressing allegiance to the King, and all who are members of a New Testament church must lose sight of selfish interests in consideration of the will of the Head of the church, who is Christ, and of what is best for the church. No one in the church or in the kingdom has any right to exalt himself above the King of the kingdom and the Head of the church or to exalt himself to a position where equality of authority with Christ is sought or claimed.

Another similarity between the church and the kingdom has to do with the ideals and standards for the members. In both the kingdom and the church high standards of righteousness should prevail.

Much is to be expected of a man who claims to be in the kingdom of God and a member of a New Testament church. "Know ye not that the unrighteous shall not inherit the kingdom of God?" (1 Cor. 6:9). A person does not get into the kingdom by deeds or works of righteousness, but he may certainly give evidence of his place in the kingdom by deeds and works of righteousness. A person does not become a member of a church by being good, but he can greatly strengthen the influence of the church by the manner in which he lives for the Lord. The kingdom of God is characterized by righteousness. "The kingdom of God is . . . righteousness" (Rom. 14:17). Righteousness is the very symbol of the Lord's reign over his people. "But unto the Son he saith, Thy throne, O God, is for ever and ever: a sceptre of righteousness is the sceptre of thy kingdom" (Heb. 1:8).

Unrighteousness has no place in the kingdom of God. Jesus said, "Except your righteousness shall exceed the righteousness of the scribes and Pharisees, ye shall in no case enter into the kingdom of heaven" (Matt. 5:20). While the appeals for righteousness are made with reference to the kingdom of God, the same high standards of righteousness are called for in the churches.

To the church at Thessalonica Paul makes this appeal, as he charged and exhorted them "that ye would walk worthy of God, who hath called you unto his kingdom and glory" (1 Thess. 2:12). In the churches the members are to walk, talk, and live like citizens of the kingdom of God, and it is a part of the business of the church to help them to do this. To the church at Rome Paul writes, "Be not overcome of evil, but overcome evil with good" (Rom. 12:21).

As a fourth similarity between the churches and the kingdom, we wish to consider one which is overlooked by many—that of their present realities. This important fact deserves lengthy consideration for a clear presentation. To be sure, most people accept this as the church age. It is generally accepted even among the strong dispensationalists, but the kingdom of God is also a present, current reality. The kingdom must not be reserved until some future date and then be conceived of only as a semispiritual, semipolitical, and material kingdom where Jesus shall reign from Jerusalem. He is now at the head of his kingdom.

There are numerous references in Matthew, Mark, and Luke to the fact that the kingdom of heaven is at hand (Matt. 3:2; 4:17; 10:7; Mark 1:15; Luke 10:9,11). The more accurate translation from these passages is, "The kingdom of God [or the kingdom of heaven] has come near." In the light of the fact that Jesus in his teachings calls for a present and current repentance and makes the kingdom of God a motive for repentance, it would seem that he intended to teach the kingdom as a present reality. Surely Jesus would not have commanded the Jews to repent on the grounds of a kingdom that was removed some two thousand years from them to a time when he should come again to the earth. The idea seems to be that they must repent not in order to bring the kingdom near but that they were to repent because the kingdom was already at hand and ready to be entered upon gospel terms.

According to Jesus, the kingdom must have already been in existence. There is a reference which indicates that the kingdom was in existence in the days of John the Baptist as well as during the earthly ministry of Jesus. "From the days of John the Baptist until now the kingdom of heaven suffereth violence, and the violent take it by force" (Matt. 11:12). An explanation of this passage is not attempted here, but it is quoted simply to show that the kingdom of heaven was in existence.

The teachings of Christ reveal the kingdom that was in possession of qualified people during his ministry. "Blessed are the poor in spirit: for theirs is the kingdom of heaven" (Matt. 5:3). The kingdom to the poor in spirit is a present possession and not just something to be anticipated. Jesus must have regarded the kingdom as already in existence when he said, "I will give unto thee the keys of the kingdom of heaven" (Matt. 16:19). Keys to a kingdom that would not be established for centuries would not have had much meaning to the church of Jesus' day. Another familiar passage is Matthew 12:28, in which Jesus declares the presence of the kingdom: "If I cast out devils by the Spirit of God, then the kingdom of God is come unto you." There was no doubt as to the present work of Jesus in casting out demons by the Spirit of God. Such was an actual achievement of his ministry in the world. It is very simple reasoning which leads one to the conclusion that his kingdom was then with them, even while he was speaking to them.

The apostle Paul conceived of the kingdom as a present reality when he wrote to the Corinthians, "The kingdom of God is not in word, but in power" (1 Cor. 4:20). Here he is declaring that the kingdom is not just something to talk about or prophesy about, but it is a kingdom demonstrated in power and in action. According to Paul, there are certain fruits of the Spirit which constitute the kingdom of God; and where such fruits are, the kingdom of God is to be found. "The kingdom of God is not meat and drink; but righteousness, and peace, and joy in the Holy Ghost" (Rom. 14:17).

The kingdom of God is a present reality just as much as the church is in this present age, notwithstanding the fact that the kingdom of God is of a spiritual nature. There are spiritual realities just as there are material realities. For instance, the soul of man is just as real as the body of man. God is spirit, but no right-thinking person questions the reality of God. While God is invisible to the eyes of the body, he is visible to the eyes of the soul. Although the voice of God may be inaudible to the ears of the body, it is audible to the ears of the soul. In fact, God the Father, God the Son, and God the Holy Spirit are all invisible to man's natural eyes but, nonetheless, they are spiritual realities.

The Christian cannot demand or require that the kingdom of God be materialistic and political in order to be real. The spiritual realities of the kingdom of God can be far more significant than if they were only political or material. Paul said, "The things which are seen are temporal; but the things which are not seen are eternal" (2 Cor. 4:18).

At least, it is obvious in this reference that the realities of the spiritual are more lasting than the realities of the material. Those who are born of God's Spirit are endued and possessed with spiritual qualities of character and with a power to discern the things of the Spirit. The spiritual discerns the spiritual, and the spiritual receives from and responds to the spiritual. A spiritual-minded person is prepared to discover, experience, and enjoy the blessings and realities of God's kingdom today.

The person who accepts the reality of the spiritual is better prepared to live in harmony with the laws of God that are applicable to current life situations. Through believing in, depending upon, and appreciating the present reality of the spiritual aspects of God's kingdom, one is better enabled to cope with the issues of life with its multiplied demands upon us. We are told that Moses "endured, as seeing him who is invisible" (Heb. 11:27).

The kingdom of God is a present reality just as much as God is a present reality in this world. There are conditions, assurances, and evidences of the divine presence. Jesus said, "Where two or three are gathered together in my name, there am I in the midst of them" (Matt. 18:20). Those who trust in Christ as personal Saviour and Lord should be ready and willing to assert their allegiance to him as King of kings and Lord of lords. They should be willing to honor him as the Master of their lives or as the sovereign Ruler.

Strictly speaking, a kingdom is composed of a king and his subjects, who are devoted to the interests, program, principles, and policies of the king. This can begin with a king and one subject and multiply and extend to the king and many subjects, with the subjects as integral and component parts of the kingdom administering the affairs of the king with abiding loyalty.

A well-known attribute of God is his omnipresence. In a general way we believe in the all-present God; but in a specific and more personal way we may experience his presence and engage in activities within his kingdom in the consciousness of his presence. In a general sense God is present in the universe, but in a much more real and personal way he is present in his kingdom and is revealing himself to his children in the kingdom. Believers in Christ are called in the Scriptures "kings and priests" and "a royal priesthood" (Rev. 5:10; 1 Peter 2:9). This is true of the believers in each generation since the days of our Lord on earth.

When Jesus said, "My kingdom is not of this world" (John 18:36), he was not saying that his kingdom is not *in* the world; neither was he saying that his kingdom has no functions in the world, no representatives, no evidence, and no manifestation in the world.

The kingdom as a present reality may be emphasized in the fact that there is a very real sense in which Jesus is reigning as the King in his kingdom today. If the kingdom of God be in you, which it cannot be unless Christ is in you, then Jesus must be even now enthroned in the heart life. Jesus called himself the "Lord and Master" in speaking to his disciples (John 13:14). "One is your Master, even Christ" (Matt. 23:8). Peter on the day of Pentecost proclaimed him as Lord: "Therefore let all the house of Israel know assuredly, that God hath made that same Jesus, whom ye have crucified, both Lord and Christ" (Acts 2:36).

Christ is now the King in the hearts of those who trust him fully as Saviour and have surrendered to him as Lord, and he now with authority directs the lives of his people who are his kingdom subjects. His dominion is in the realm of those who have yielded to him as Lord. It is the kingdom of love and light, of righteousness and truth in which he reigns in individual hearts. The present realities of the kingdom are not dependent upon numbers, race, geography, or externals of any kind. Wherever and whenever the Lord Jesus is trusted, obeyed, honored, and glorified by those who have received him, experienced him, and enthroned him, we find the realities of the kingdom of God.

The disciples of Jesus heralded him as the King in his royal entrance into Jerusalem shortly before his crucifixion. Jesus accepted the title of king, which they so fittingly bestowed upon him. "Blessed be the King that cometh in the name of the Lord: peace in heaven, and glory in the highest" (Luke 19:38). In answering the critical Pharisees, he said, "If these should hold their peace, the stones would immediately cry out" (Luke 19:40). Apparently Jesus was pleased with being honored as the King.

Before his ascension Jesus claimed all of the powers of king in his introduction to the Great Commission, as he said: "All power is given unto me in heaven and in earth" (Matt. 28:18).

In a post-resurrection message to his churches our Lord and King speaks from his throne in heaven as a present King. "To him that overcometh will I grant to sit with me in my throne, even as I also overcame, and am set down with my Father in his throne" (Rev. 3:21). He is revealing himself as already on his throne in heaven after his ascension, in connection with his exaltation. The apostle Paul under divine inspiration wrote of the Christ who is now at the right hand of God. "Seek those things which are above, where Christ sitteth on the right hand of God" (Col. 3:1).

When Stephen, the first Christian martyr, was dying, he testified, "I see the heavens opened, and the Son of man standing on the right hand of God" (Acts 7:56). Some have said that Christ

arose from his seat on the throne to better behold, and to pay
tribute to, the first Christian martyr, who was now dying so nobly
for the cause of Christ.

Jesus our Lord is King today of spiritual Israel, but this is not to
be confused with national Israel. He was never anointed to be the
king over some political or temporal power. He is as much the
King of the believing Gentiles as he is the King of the believing
Jews. There is but one kingdom and there is but one King, and
God is no respecter of persons when it comes to those who enter
his kingdom; they must all come to him through his Son, Jesus
Christ. The King presupposes the kingdom, and the kingdom calls
for the King.

The continued presence of so much sin in the world must not
cause God's people to despair and to assume for one moment
that Jesus has abdicated his throne. We are still living in a world
of free moral agents in which men make their choices, all too often
without regard to the Saviour of men, the Son of righteousness
and the King of glory. Someone has suggested that Christ reigns
in this sinful world today somewhat as the sun reigns in the
heavens. Sometimes there are clouds to intercept our view, and
always there is a certain amount of darkness, but somewhere the
sun still shines to dispel the darkness and to warm the frigid air.

John the Baptist preached the gospel of the kingdom, and
Jesus preached the gospel of the kingdom. "And Jesus went about
all Galilee, teaching in their synagogues, and preaching the gospel of the kingdom" (Matt. 4:23). "And Jesus went about all the
cities and villages, teaching in their synagogues, and preaching
the gospel of the kingdom" (Matt. 9:35).

The twelve were sent out to preach the kingdom of God. "Then
he called his twelve disciples together. . . . And he sent them
to preach the kingdom of God" (Luke 9:1-2). The gospel of
the kingdom is to be preached in all of the world; and it is the responsibility of the church in this present age to do this. Jesus said,
"And this gospel of the kingdom shall be preached in all the
world for a witness unto all nations; and then shall the end come"
(Matt. 24:14). There is but one gospel for one world.

Jesus comforted, challenged, and encouraged the little group of disciples in his day with the promise of the kingdom. "Fear not, little flock; for it is your Father's good pleasure to give you the kingdom" (Luke 12:32). The kingdom of God deserved priority in the lives of the followers of Jesus in his day, and it deserves priority in our day. And how could Jesus require priority for something that did not exist? "Seek ye first the kingdom of God, and his righteousness; and all these things shall be added unto you" (Matt. 6:33). There is a current responsibility to pray for the prosperity of the kingdom in our day, even as the disciples of Jesus were taught to pray for the kingdom that it might be more real and more effective. "Thy kingdom come. Thy will be done in earth, as it is in heaven" (Matt. 6:10). God's people in New Testament days had already received the kingdom, and the kingdom was used as the basis of an appeal for more acceptable service.

"Wherefore we receiving a kingdom which cannot be moved, let us have grace, whereby we may serve God acceptably with reverence and godly fear" (Heb. 12:28). Jesus taught that there were some who heard him teach and who were associated with him that should see the kingdom in their own time in the world. "But I tell you of a truth, there be some standing here, which shall not taste of death, till they see the kingdom of God" (Luke 9:27).

If the twenty-fourth Psalm is a prophecy of Christ's glorious return to heaven after his atoning death and triumphant resurrection, as it seems to be, then how real is his reign now? "Lift up your heads, O ye gates; even lift them up, ye everlasting doors; and the King of glory shall come in. Who is this King of glory? The Lord of hosts, he is the King of glory" (Psalm 24:9–10).

Our King is the present King, "who is the blessed and only Potentate, the King of kings, and Lord of lords" (1 Tim. 6:15). He is the eternal King, who is to be glorified in his people through the churches in this present age. "Now unto the King eternal, immortal, invisible, the only wise God, be honour and glory for ever and ever" (1 Tim. 1:17). In a very real sense the church age and the kingdom age are parallel in this age, with the church as the agent of the kingdom.

Surely we are not willing to delay the kingdom until some future time and as Gentiles make the same error with reference to Christ's Second Coming that the Jews made in his first coming. The Jews tried to make a political, material, temporal reign out of Christ's first coming and rejected him when he failed to measure up to their expectations. Shall the Gentiles be as guilty in rejecting him if he fails to set up in his Second Coming some sort of a kingdom in Jerusalem from which he will rule over a kingdom that will be more physical, material, and political than spiritual? Christ is reigning now in the hearts of those who are surrendered to him, and "he must reign, till he hath put all enemies under his feet. The last enemy that shall be destroyed is death" (1 Cor. 15:25–26).

The similarity between the church and the kingdom in connection with the program and growth of each is obvious. The ideal would be to follow the pattern set forth in Acts 2:47, where we are told that "the Lord added to the church daily such as should be saved." The growth of the kingdom and the growth of the church should be somewhat simultaneous, as is indicated here. That is, the growth would be always the same in each one, if everyone who is saved would follow the Lord in baptism and church membership and if everyone who unites with the church were truly in the kingdom of God first.

The growth should be the same in both the church and the kingdom if it measures up to the ideal of the Scriptures. The program and business of the church and the kingdom must be similar, with the church as a visible manifestation of the kingdom and as the instrument, agent, arm, or servant of the kingdom. The mission of both church and kingdom must be redemptive.

The message of both church and kingdom must be one that is Christ-centered. It must be one which presents Christ in his person as the eternal Son of God, "the only begotten of the Father, full of grace and truth" (John 1:14). The message of church and kingdom must be one which presents Christ as the one and only Saviour and Lord. It must exalt Christ in his glorious pre-existence, his miraculous birth, his sinless life, his atoning death, his victorious resurrection, his ascension and exaltation, his continuous intercession, and his personal and imminent return.

The means for the extension of the Lord's work must be by the power of the Holy Spirit—enduing the servants of the Lord for the execution of their assignments, accompanying the gospel message, applying the same in convicting power upon the hearts of the unregenerate, drawing them to Christ, and making the penitent and trusting ones new creatures in Christ.

The motivating force of both church and kingdom is love for the Lord and love for one another. Paul wrote, "For the love of Christ constraineth us" (2 Cor. 5:14). Other motives are low and unworthy.

The same purpose must characterize the program of the church and of the kingdom—that of glorifying God. "Unto him be glory in the church by Christ Jesus throughout all ages, world without end" (Eph. 3:21). The church and the kingdom must both be a force for God and for good now. This is as much the kingdom age now as it is the church age. This is the age of the gospel. This is the age of the Holy Spirit, but the church, through the aid of the Holy Spirit, is promoting the work of the kingdom by propagating the one gospel of Christ, which includes the gospel of the kingdom.

If we would try to be dispensational, we would say that *now* is the time to evangelize the lost world; *now* is the time to win lost souls to Christ; *now* is the time to pray for, and rely upon, the power of the Holy Spirit; and *now* is the time to conserve the results of evangelism through the program of the church.

Thus may be recognized the similarities between the church and the kingdom. While they are not identical, there is no conflict between the kingdom of God and the New Testament church, and there ought to be great harmony between them. Both the church and the kingdom must grow. Some of the same requirements and laws of growth are possessed by the two.

The church grew from a very small beginning in the time of Christ until there were churches scattered over the then known world by the end of the first century. It seems that the churches had their most rapid growth during the first century, which, of course, proves that the major factor for growth is the power of the Holy Spirit, because they did not have facilities such as we have today from a human point of view. The Jerusalem church is known as the mother church, and indeed it did become the mother of many churches. The scattered believers were organized into many churches, and Paul soon was able to refer to them as "the churches of Galatia" (Gal. 1:2). Likewise, the kingdom had a small beginning but has experienced mighty growth. Many of the parables of Jesus depict the growth of the kingdom in his day as well as predicting something of its future growth, which is illustrated in the parable of the mustard seed (Matt. 13:31–32) and the parable of the leaven (Matt. 13:33).

We may also look to the future for the similarity between the churches and the kingdom. Some day in the future the saved of all the ages of all the world will be gathered together in the eternal heavenly home. This general assembly in heaven is the church of the future. It is the church of the first-born, about which we read in Hebrews 12:23.

This church in heaven will then be the same as the kingdom, but it will not include any of the unsaved people who are on the church rolls. The church in heaven, unfortunately, will not be the same as the total membership of all the churches and is not likely to be the same as the total membership of any one church. The Lord of glory, the King of the kingdom, the Head of the church will be the central figure in heaven. This will be the hour for the church and kingdom victorious and the hour for the church and kingdom glorious.

Only the saved shall be in that *ekklēsia,* and it will be altogether spiritual, merged with the kingdom. The two shall then be synonymous. The church then will have triumphed over all her foes, and the perpetuity of the church shall be as real as the perpetuity of the kingdom. The members of the *ekklēsia* in heaven will have completely sanctified and glorified bodies and souls, as the mortal becomes immortal, the corruptible becomes incorruptible, and the earthly becomes heavenly.

Four

The Churches as the Agents of the Kingdom

SAVED PEOPLE, who have the same great Saviour and the same Heavenly Father, have much in common as brothers and sisters in the family and kingdom of God. Such people find sweet fellowship with one another in worship and service and in holy conversation. They also have a compassionate concern for those who are without Christ. They soon sense the need for being associated with others of like faith and experience. Those who are truly in the kingdom of God and who have the kingdom of God in them will desire to be not only spiritually but organically joined together for the purpose of sharing their blessings with others. The kingdom of God does, undoubtedly, manifest itself in and through the New Testament churches as the agents of the kingdom.

Autonomous groups of born-again people voluntarily and obediently associated together for the propagation of the message and work of their Lord certainly do constitute agencies as well as evidences of the kingdom. Since the nature of the kingdom is spiritual, there follows an inevitable need for the churches to be spiritual and for God's people in his churches to live consecrated lives of consistent devotion to our Lord. Anything about any church that fails to make spiritual contributions in harmony with the spiritual nature of the kingdom of God should be eliminated.

When Jesus said in Matthew 16:19, "I will give unto thee the keys of the kingdom of heaven," he must not have been speaking or thinking of the church and the kingdom's being the same thing, or he would have used the word "church," as in verse 18. He evidently was then engaged in the process of establishing or building his church; but even at this time the kingdom of heaven was an abiding reality. There were policies, purposes, and provisions established in the kingdom of heaven which must antedate or precede the administration of the affairs of the church upon earth. A more literal and more accurate translation of Matthew 16:19 than that of the King James Version would seem to be: "Whatsoever thou shalt bind on earth *shall have already been bound in heaven:* and whatsoever thou shalt loose on earth *shall have already been loosed in heaven.*"

For every divinely appointed activity and program of the church upon the earth there is to be found a heavenly precedent and pattern. The churches are not engaged in the business of initiating or originating plans and policies for the kingdom of heaven, but of discerning, administering, and executing that which is of heavenly origin.

With our citizenship in heaven, according to Philippians 3:20 (ASV), the churches are as colonies of heaven to carry out heaven's program upon earth. They are charged with the propagation and administration of the affairs of the kingdom of heaven upon earth. The churches have heavenly privileges, heavenly functions, and heavenly responsibilities. The program of the church does not originate within the church or by church decrees. The program of the church has its origin in heaven. The pattern and the principles for the entire program of the church are established and ordered in heaven and simply projected upon the earth. The churches have the privilege then of using the keys of the kingdom for kingdom purposes and in harmony with kingdom plans.

To his churches Christ has given the authority and responsibility of carrying on his work. The churches are to announce from him the terms or conditions upon which he will forgive sins. To the churches have been given the keys of the kingdom, consisting of the Word of God as the saving message of Christ, and the Holy Spirit. Some might include the privilege of prayer as another one of the keys. Wherever the keys of the kingdom are used, God has opened the doors of the kingdom to receive penitent, trusting sinners. His churches have been charged with the responsibility of carrying out his worldwide program of evangelization. The evangelized have not been completely instructed until they have been taught the precepts and examples of their Lord and have been led to obey him.

The program of the churches as the agents of the kingdom must harmonize with the kingdom. One cannot divorce the program of the churches from the kingdom of God. The churches may truly be regarded as the agents, arms, and instruments of the kingdom for the advancement and extension of the kingdom in harmony with kingdom principles, methods, and motives. There can be harmony without identity. The bass, the tenor, the alto, and the soprano may all harmonize in the quartet for one purpose, that of making melody unto the Lord, but they are still not the same voices and not the same parts. These four parts may also blend with an accompanying organ and piano, but they are not all the same as the organ and the piano. The various instruments of a large orchestra may harmoniously and beautifully blend together under the able direction of the master, but they are not the same instruments; yet together they may well constitute the over-all instrument of the director, who is responsible for their acceptable rendition. God always blesses the churches in their ministry when they function as the agents of his kingdom. Indeed, the church functioned mightily as the agent of the kingdom on the day of Pentecost by proclaiming the word of God and exalting the crucified and risen Lord under the direction of, and in the power of, the Holy Spirit. The churches are completely dependent upon the Holy Spirit for power and guidance.

The church was not only functioning on the day of Pentecost as the agent of the kingdom, but there was a powerful manifestation of the kingdom. The church had waited in prayer for ten days, and the promise of Christ was fulfilled as the Holy Spirit descended upon the church in mighty power. The day of Pentecost demonstrates what Paul wrote to the Corinthians: "For the kingdom of God is not in word, but in power" (1 Cor. 4:20).

The church is designed for kingdom purposes. Christ is the founder, foundation, owner, and occupant. Every particular congregation should be the agent of the kingdom of God upon earth. Dr. George W. McDaniel, in his book *The Churches of the New Testament,* says of the New Testament church as a particular congregation that "it means the regenerate persons in a locality who unite themselves voluntarily together in conforming with Christ's laws for *establishing his kingdom* in the earth." A particular church has for its primary mission the propagation of the gospel, and it is, therefore, basic in the spread of the gospel. Wherever Paul went preaching the gospel to the lost and winning them to Christ, he never considered his work finished until he had led them to organize a church for the continuation of that which had been begun.

The church should be regarded as a group of baptized believers in Christ who have covenanted to carry out the commands of their Lord, the Head of the church. His authoritative commission is to "Go." The churches have a divine mission to evangelize the world, to baptize the saved who are willing to become members of the church, and to teach them to observe all of the commands of their Lord.

The question of Christ's authority is a very penetrating and searching one. "Why call ye me, Lord, Lord, and do not the things which I say?" (Luke 6:46)

The churches, as the agents of the kingdom, have a definite privilege and responsibility in this sinful world. We read in Revelation where the lampstand refers to the church: "The seven candlesticks [lampstands] . . . are the seven churches" (Rev. 1:20). The churches are to be light-bearers to those in darkness. Our lights as individuals should shine most lustrously through his churches for the glory of God. The candlesticks constitute an apt figure of speech for the churches as agents of the kingdom, suggesting the very means of conveying it to others. As the churches are the custodians of the gospel, so are they the depositories for its light. They are at once the recipients and the disseminators of the light of the gospel. It is the responsibility of the churches to extend the invitation for entrance into the kingdom of heaven. It is not voided because many reject it.

The message must emphasize the accessibility of the kingdom. "The kingdom of heaven is at hand [has come nigh]" (Matt. 3:2). When Jesus sent out the twelve apostles, he told them to preach the same message. "And as ye go, preach, saying, The kingdom of heaven is at hand" (Matt. 10:7). According to Mark 1:14, Jesus himself preached "the kingdom of God."

If Jesus' forerunner and the herald of his coming preached this message of the kingdom of God, and if Jesus preached it and commissioned his followers to preach it, then surely the church has the same responsibility for proclaiming the message. Christ preached more on the theme of the kingdom of God than upon any other subject. He said, "I must preach the kingdom of God to other cities also: for therefore am I sent" (Luke 4:43). "And it came to pass afterward, that he went throughout every city and village, preaching and shewing the glad tidings of the kingdom of God: and the twelve were with him" (Luke 8:1).

In the church's responsibility of evangelizing the world, the message of evangelism is linked vitally with the kingdom of God. John the Baptist came preaching, "Repent ye: for the kingdom of heaven is at hand" (Matt. 3:2). Jesus took up the same message and launched his public ministry by preaching upon this theme: "Repent: for the kingdom of heaven is at hand" (Matt. 4:17). Later Jesus said in an evangelistic message to Nicodemus, "Except a man be born again, he cannot see the kingdom of God" (John 3:3).

The program of New Testament churches should be the program of the kingdom of God on earth. Pointing people to Christ, the Saviour and King, is the chief business of every saved person.

The churches have a responsibility to provide an atmosphere that is conducive for winning the lost to Christ. The praying, teaching, preaching, and training program of the church should emphasize, magnify, and promote the work of soul-winning.

God's kingdom is advanced only in proportion to the interest that is created and manifested in pointing sinners to "the Lamb of God, which taketh away the sin of the world." The churches should major on preparing, inspiring, and challenging God's people to tell others about Jesus and his power to save and keep. "Let him know, that he which converteth the sinner from the error of his way shall save a soul from death, and shall hide a multitude of sins" (James 5:20). Someone has well said that the ideal of the kingdom of heaven is in the words taken from the model prayer of our Lord for his disciples: "Thy kingdom come. Thy will be done in earth, as it is in heaven" (Matt. 6:10). The will of God must be interpreted in terms of evangelism. It was his will that Jesus should die for the sins of the world, and his atoning death on the cross constitutes the very heart of the gospel. When Jesus prayed in Gethsemane's garden, "Not my will, but thine, be done," he accepted the will of God for him to die for the sins of the world. God's will is that men shall know and meet the terms of salvation. Peter declares concerning his will that he is "not willing that any should perish, but that all should come to repentance" (2 Peter 3:9).

The pattern of soul-winning was definitely set in the early churches. The number of people won to Christ on a percentage basis as per number of members was far greater than any percentage that the churches can claim today. Those who were scattered abroad by the persecution in Jerusalem went everywhere preaching the gospel. The churches of the first century carried the gospel to all parts of the Roman Empire. The early apostles were accused of turning the world upside down, and as they did so, they were turning it right side up, which is the only way that Christ can be on the throne.

Most people will readily admit that very little of the Lord's work would be going on anywhere were it not for his churches.

In the churches the children of God are given the cultivation for their Christian lives; their talents are developed, harnessed, and utilized in kingdom service. There is a great difference between the unprotected, the uncultivated, and the undernourished Christian outside the church and the one who receives the care of the church and its ministry. What a difference there is in both the quantity and the quality of fruit borne by the person in the kingdom and in the church, as compared with the one in the kingdom but not in the church!

The churches have the definite responsibility of constantly providing a home for new converts that is aimed toward their healthy growth in Christian life and character. Spiritual warmth is essential to the good care of newborn souls. Just as there are incubator babies in some of our hospitals, so there may be a need for some spiritual incubation for new converts, especially among those who are saved before they have any background for the living of the Christian life.

Many new Christians do not get off to a good start either because they fail to affiliate immediately with the church or because the church fails to minister to them on the basis of their needs. The church usually will seem to each individual what he himself is. The spiritual temperature of the church will be to the individual about what his own spiritual temperature is. Some people are so cold-natured physically that sometimes they think they are about to freeze to death in a room that may be fairly comfortable for others. There are others who are so warm-natured that they are too warm in rooms that are comfortable to those around them.

The writer was holding a meeting in a rural church, where the spiritual tides were at least normal, and God was blessing in a manner for which many were humbly grateful. Into the meeting one night came a backslidden member who had been living the life of a recluse. It was the one and only service which he attended, but he diagnosed the situation that evening in line with his own condition as he called the visiting preacher to one side to tell him what the trouble was with the church. Said he,

"Preacher, I'll tell you what the trouble with this church is—it's just cold and droopy—cold and droopy—that's what it is."

The churches do have a responsibility toward every member, and especially toward those who are weak in the faith and who need special care and constant spiritual warmth. R. G. Lee frequently has been heard to say that "too many of our churches are like floating sepulchers manned by frozen crews." The churches have the responsibility of seeing that no citizen of the kingdom suffers from malnutrition. The Word of God is essential to the diet of growing Christians. God's Word is referred to in the Scriptures as milk, bread, and meat. All of these are important to proper nourishment. There are many half-starved Christians, who either are not partaking of what is available or they are being fed a starvation diet where the Word of God has been so diluted as to produce anemic Christians.

The churches, as the agents of the kingdom, must provide a program for adequately teaching and preaching the Word of God as the basic diet for the children of the kingdom. The churches have the responsibility for constantly providing an adequate number of trained teachers for imparting spiritual truths through every phase of the church program. Ministers from the pulpit do well to remember that the waiting people in the congregation are hungry for the Word of God and will go away empty and hungry, with an aching void, and spiritually weak if they fail to hear the exposition of the Word of God.

While spiritual warmth and a spiritual diet are so very important to the growth of the citizens of the kingdom, proper exercise is another basic factor in growth. The churches also have a responsibility in providing challenging and appropriate means for the exercise of God's people. Paul said, "Exercise thyself . . . unto godliness" (1 Tim. 4:7).

There are, perhaps, some saved people and church members who never have been asked to do anything beyond what the pastor said when they presented themselves for membership, which was, "Be seated." What a sad commentary it would be to stop at the point of telling a new convert to be seated! The churches might well take a statement from Jesus, when he said to his disciples, *"Arise,* let us go hence" (John 14:31). Spiritual food should provide spiritual strength, and spiritual strength is to be exerted in constructive channels of service. The churches must encourage an exercise unto godliness, which is not only an inward growth of character but also an outward expression of service.

There are too many "fattening hog" type of Christians, who like to eat and loaf around the throne but never really engage in any vital exercise for the Lord. The fattening hogs are kept confined in close quarters and exercise is discouraged, while food and water are always kept before them. The aim, of course, is to let all of the food value go to fat. With the many types of meetings in the churches for preaching, teaching, and feeding, caution needs to be taken against letting the people feel that their chief mission has been accomplished within the confines of the church, where they may so often feed their souls. The main task lies ahead and outside the walls of the church building, where strength may be gained from everyday exercise unto godliness, which is important to the kingdom. The larger ministry of the church is far beyond what goes on in the building itself.

The man who is always feeding his body on rich food and never exercises sufficiently is soon the victim of fatness and flabbiness. His muscles turn to fat. He has no real strength, vitality, or resistance. He is not worth as much in carrying a load, or in climbing a hill, or descending into the valley below as the quality and quantity of his nourishment should provide. So it is with Christians. The nourishment received, the inspiration and instructions given should be utilized in the realm of applied religion.

While environment, diet, and exercise are included in the ministry of the church as the agent of the kingdom in behalf of its citizens, nothing much has been said about those who seem to have no appetite for what is provided. The church owes these some special concern.

The anxious mother is always concerned for the health of the child who has no appetite for the kind of food that is needed.

Some little children want sweets many times a day. There are some youngsters who refuse to eat meat. Others refuse vegetables and fruits that contain important vitamins. There are some who have a difficult time in making the transition from the soft, creamed baby foods to the more solid diet that requires some chewing. Some children scarcely will eat unless someone hand-feeds them. Yet others lose their appetites and refuse their food with the slightest disturbance. These are parables on the care that some little ones in the kingdom expect and require at the hands of the church.

When the children of Israel were wandering on their way toward the Land of Promise, they manifested so much of the instability of human nature among God's children. At first, they cried for food from heaven. Not much later, they lost their appetites and revolted against what was being provided. "And the people spake against God, and against Moses, Wherefore have ye brought us up out of Egypt to die in the wilderness? for there is no bread, neither is there any water; and our soul loatheth this light bread" (Num. 21:5). Through disobedience, a lack of faith, a dissatisfaction with God's leader Moses, the children of Israel lost their appetite for what was being provided, and they lusted again for the things of Egypt. They longed again for the fleshpots of Egypt. "We remember the fish, which we did eat in Egypt freely; the cucumbers, and the melons, and the leeks, and the onions, and the garlick: But now our soul is dried away: there is nothing at all, beside this manna, before our eyes" (Num. 11:5-6).

So often professing Christians and church members, through disobedience, a lack of faith, and a dissatisfaction with God's leaders, lose their appetites for the diet of the soul and become spiritual weaklings, objects of the special care of the church in prayer, patience, and painstaking efforts to present the claims of the Lord upon his wayward people.

The whole program of the churches should be such as to strengthen the reign of Christ in the hearts of God's children and to make them more loyal citizens of the kingdom of God, as well as advance the kingdom through winning new converts.

The churches must proclaim the message of sanctification, although they do not have sanctification within themselves. The churches must proclaim the doctrine of perseverance, although they do not have perseverance within themselves. That is to say, just joining a church certainly will not provide salvation, sanctification, and perseverance.

The churches have the high and holy privilege of voluntarily co-operating in kingdom work without the necessity of organic union and without the necessity of having some superecclesiastical organization to impose authority upon the autonomy of the churches.

Churches of unlike faith and order may have difficulty in co-operating along many lines, but churches of like faith and order may accomplish great things in the kingdom of God on a co-operative basis. There is much effective work that can be done through a co-operative effort that one particular church alone could never accomplish. Voluntary co-operation does not call for the surrender of the autonomy of the church. A church can exercise its autonomy in a congregational vote to co-operate in the missionary and benevolent program of the many churches just as well as it could take a negative vote to refuse to co-operate. The positive is always more constructive than the negative and represents a higher degree of development. No one church may be strong enough to launch and maintain a successful missionary program in all of the world, but all of the churches of like faith and order may support a worthy mission program all over the world as they pool their resources. The task of advancing the kingdom of God is great enough to challenge all of our churches to join hand and heart in making Christ known to the whole world.

All New Testament churches are under the same Great Commission of the Lord. Surely, if they recognize and honor the same authoritative commission, they ought also to be able to employ common motives in propagating a common gospel, as they accept the principle of voluntary co-operation as "labourers together with God" (1 Cor. 3:9). If they can be partners with God in a worldwide kingdom enterprise, they ought also to be able to work as partners with the children of God who accept the responsibilities of partnership with the one and only God, their Heavenly Father and the Father of their one and only Saviour, the Lord Jesus Christ.

If they can all do on a co-operative basis, in the kingdom of God and for the kingdom, that which they cannot do separately, such may logically be interpreted as an increased loyalty to the kingdom.

The sphere of influence and the area of autonomy are greatly enhanced through voluntary participation in a program of co-operation. By this means a particular church is extending its ministry far beyond the confines of the local congregation and far beyond the limits of the community where the church is located. Instead of autonomy being circumscribed by the limitations of a small area occupied by resident members of the church, the autonomy declares itself in favor of that which lets the people on the other side of the world know that somewhere there are New Testament churches that are taking the Commission of the Lord seriously.

There is such a thing as an individual or a church's imprisoning and enslaving itself through selfishly imposed restrictions in an effort to assert autonomy that results in having little or no part in kingdom work beyond the four walls of the church building.

When New Testament churches voluntarily contribute their mission money through co-operative programs, the funds thus given become a part of the funds given by thousands of churches of like faith and order, and all of the co-operating churches together determine the use of the funds. By this procedure the particular church has a voice, not only over the few hundred dollars it gives, but its voice is expanded and extended in this co-operative endeavor until it exercises its autonomy in the disposition of millions of dollars for the work of the kingdom.

The church, as the agent of the kingdom, is to be militant. Each New Testament church is a part of the great army of our Lord. The church must be the aggressor in this world of sin. The church must assume the offensive. Enemy territory must be invaded and claimed for Christ. Halfhearted, apologetic methods and attitudes will not accomplish the task. There must be a positive program of advance in which the word "retreat" is foreign. The correct translation of Matthew 16:18 places the church upon the offensive. "And the gates of hell shall not withstand the attack of the church" gives a better understanding of the church's overrunning the fields of sin as the church enters enemy territory with the saving message of Christ. All of the powers of the enemy cannot stop the onward march of God's people when they are marching under the banner of the cross in obedience to their Lord's command and with the gospel message that is God's power unto salvation.

Any apparent failures in the conquests of the kingdom through the churches have not been the result of the overwhelming power of the devil or of the weakness of our King, but rather have come from the failures, indifference, and disloyalty on the part of the subjects of his kingdom.

The churches have no alternative but to go forward under the marching orders of their King. The democratic feature of the church does not imply that the members can ever scripturally vote to do anything contrary to their King. These democracies must function under the King, and his orders must not be trifled with, set aside, or disobeyed. Indeed, the church is the custodian and the administrator of the affairs of the kingdom of God.

The New Testament church is a visible, audible, tangible manifestation of the invisible, inaudible, intangible kingdom of God; but because of man's carnality and the kingdom's spirituality, the church cannot be a perfected manifestation of the kingdom. Nevertheless, the church is the unique, exclusive, divinely established, divinely authorized agent of the kingdom of God.

While primary emphasis cannot be placed upon this point, it does, however, seem appropriate to consider briefly some of the more practical, and even social, aspects of the church as the agent of the kingdom of God. Here it must be ever kept in mind that the unit of a Christian society is a redeemed, regenerated individual committed to the will of God. It must also be remembered that there is no such thing as the brotherhood of man apart from the fatherhood of God, and there is no such thing as the fatherhood of God apart from being children of God through faith in Jesus Christ. The kind of tree determines the kind of fruit. There will be a better society, better homes, better schools, better communities, better government, better living conditions, and a better understanding among people only in proportion to their acceptance of Jesus Christ as personal Saviour and Lord. The churches as the agents of the kingdom will contribute to a better world only in proportion to the production of better individuals, which can come only through transformed hearts and lives by the saving grace of God in Christ.

The churches must continue with unswerving, unwavering fidelity to the one gospel for one world. The churches are not the agents of the kingdom for propagating many gospels, such as the social gospel, the gospel of the kingdom today, the gospel of the kingdom of the future, Paul's special gospel, the gospel of the kingdom of heaven, the gospel of the kingdom of God, and the gospel of the grace of God. The one gospel may have aspects related to all of the above, but when all has been said and done, the churches have but one gospel for one world, and that is the gospel of redeeming grace through the crucified, buried, risen, ascended, returning eternal Son of God.

Five

Citizenship in the Kingdom

FOR OUR CITIZENSHIP is in heaven" (Phil. 3:20, ASV). The stability and security of the Roman world at this time filled the thoughts of the people with high conceptions of citizenship values. This citizenship idea must have appealed especially to the Philippians, who took pride in their Roman citizenship. Many times Paul had found his Roman citizenship to be a good protection for himself. The citizenship idea had been adopted by the Jews from Greek civic life long before this letter was written.

The heavenly citizenship need never conflict with our being good citizens of our country, inasmuch as Jesus teaches a nonconflicting loyalty: "Render therefore unto Caesar the things which are Caesar's; and unto God the things that are God's" (Matt. 22:21).

This newer version of Philippians 3:20 is an improved translation and gives more meaning to the verse than the King James Version, which is, "For our conversation is in heaven" (Phil. 3:20). This would make God's children here in this world as colonies of heaven with allegiance to our King, the Lord Jesus Christ, and with loyalty to the kingdom of God. As such, they are looking after the business of the kingdom of God while they are here in this world. They are projections of the kingdom of God upon earth and subjects of the King and the laws of his kingdom. At the same time, they enjoy the protection that is provided for all of the citizens of the kingdom of God.

The fact that citizenship is in heaven is further illustrated by the statement that we are "strangers and pilgrims on the earth" (Heb. 11:13). Our real loyalties and interests are in the kingdom of heaven. Paul's reference to being "ambassadors for Christ" (2 Cor. 5:20) further illustrates the fact of citizenship in heaven. An ambassador is one who represents his king at the court of another.

The sinful nature of fallen man cannot inherit the kingdom of God. Man is not by nature a child of God or a child of the kingdom. He is unfit for the kingdom of God apart from the spiritual birth. The spiritual life, akin to God, does not begin until there has been the birth from above. All are by nature the "children of wrath."

To become a Christian is to become a child of God, and to become a child of God is to be born of God. The acceptance by faith of Jesus Christ as personal Saviour is at the center of such a transaction and of such an experience. "But as many as received him, to them gave he power to become the sons of God, even to them that believe on his name: Which were born, not of blood, nor of the will of the flesh, nor of the will of man, but of God" (John 1:12–13). "Whosoever believeth that Jesus is the Christ is born of God" (1 John 5:1).

What a tremendous and significant change is wrought in the lives of those who become citizens of the kingdom of God! Some of the world's greatest sinners have become the world's greatest saints. The apostle Paul referred to himself in his preconversion state as being the chief of sinners. "This is a faithful saying, and worthy of all acceptation, that Christ Jesus came into the world to save sinners; of whom I am chief" (1 Tim. 1:15). Such changes are not to be explained by the psychologists, scientists, philosophers, rationalists, intellectualists, or theologians apart from the regenerating power of the Holy Spirit. The change is not the result of legislation, reformation, emulation, education, or civilization, but of *regeneration*. The regenerating, transforming power of God has been at work in changing one from the child of the devil to the child of God.

The statement on regeneration from *The Baptist Faith and Message* may help better to present this experience which puts one in the kingdom of God. "Regeneration or the new birth is a change of heart wrought by the Holy Spirit, whereby we become partakers of the divine nature and a holy disposition is given, leading to the love and practice of righteousness. It is a work of God's free grace conditioned upon faith in Christ and made manifest by the fruit which we bring forth to the glory of God." [1]

Concerning getting into the kingdom, the definition of repentance and faith as prerequisites to regeneration ought also to be given, and this comes from the same source.

We believe that repentance and faith are sacred duties, and also inseparable graces, wrought in our souls by the regenerating Spirit of God; whereby being deeply convinced of our guilt, danger, and helplessness, and of the way of salvation by Christ, we turn to God with unfeigned contrition, confession, and supplication for mercy; at the same time heartily receiving the Lord Jesus Christ as our Prophet, Priest, and King, and relying on him alone as the only and all-sufficient Saviour. [2]

One may be a citizen of the kingdom of heaven while yet upon earth. A good illustration of one's being a citizen of the kingdom of heaven while here in the world, and as such a part of the colony of heaven, is given by Roland Leavell.

There is a vast difference between the place Great Britain and the kingdom of Great Britain. The kingdom of Great Britain is in the hearts of all those who are loyal to the king [or queen]. A loyal subject to the king, residing in America, is yet a part of the kingdom of Great Britain. Just so, the kingdom of heaven is composed of all people who are loyal to God through faith in Jesus Christ as their Lord and King. The soul-winner seeks to lead his lost friend to enter the kingdom of

---

[1] *Op. cit.*, p. 8.
[2] *Ibid.*, pp. 8–9.

heaven here on earth, assuring him that he will enter the place heaven in the hereafter.[3]

One's relationship to the kingdom of God is conditioned upon relationship to Christ, the Son of God, the Saviour of men, who reigns in the hearts and over the lives of those who penitently trust in him as personal Saviour and Lord. Everyone who gets into his kingdom is born again and becomes a new creation. Citizens of the kingdom are enjoying a glorious experience, having been delivered from the power of darkness and translated into the kingdom of the Son of his love, with redemption and forgiveness, according to Paul (Col. 1:13–14).

The kingdom is entered through Jesus, who is the door. "I am the door: by me if any man enter in, he shall be saved" (John 10:9). God's kingdom is made up of his blood-bought children, whether they be Jew or Gentile. And all of the Jews will not be saved any more than will all of the Gentiles, although the salvation of our Lord is sufficient for all who accept Christ upon the terms of the gospel. When Paul says, "And so all Israel shall be saved" (Rom. 11:26), he must be referring to spiritual Israel since "they are not all Israel, which are of Israel" (Rom. 9:6).

Jesus said, "Behold, the kingdom of God is within you" (Luke 17:21). There are those who talk about "getting" into the kingdom and who believe that one is baptized into the kingdom. For the sake of reasoning, suppose for a moment that one is baptized into the kingdom; that still would not answer the question, "How do you get the kingdom into the man?"

Everyone who has repented of his sins toward God, personally trusted in Jesus Christ as his Saviour, and enthroned Christ in his heart as the Lord and Master of his life is making Christ his King and himself the subject of the King and is a citizen of the kingdom of God. A kingdom might well be defined as the sovereign king with a loyal subject and an administration of the affairs of the kingdom through the instrumentality of the yielded subject,

---

[3] Roland Q. Leavell, *Evangelism, Christ's Imperative Commission* (Nashville: Broadman Press, 1951), pp. 23–24.

who has voluntarily surrendered to the king out of personal choice for him above all others. In a very real sense, then, there is a miniature kingdom in the heart of every man who is the child of God through Christ and whose life is committed to Christ as Lord of his life.

This experience, this provision, and this relationship of the kingdom of God in the man produces an ideal kingdom. Where the kingdom is in the man, the man will make the interests of the kingdom uppermost in his thinking, planning, and functioning. He will be motivated by forces that operate from within rather than by forces that are superimposed from without. He will be a part of the kingdom, and the kingdom will be an integral, inseparable part of him. That produces the highly desirable condition of placing the child of God in the position of being both *in* the kingdom and *of* the kingdom. Where the kingdom of God is in the man and the man lives in harmony with kingdom laws, he will be representing the kingdom wherever he goes and become a part of the kingdom's expansion as he spreads its influence.

The regenerated individual thus becomes the true unit of the kingdom of God. What about the character of the kingdom citizen? The kingdom citizen is a new creature in Christ and should so conduct himself. "Therefore if any man be in Christ, he is a new creature: old things are passed away; behold, all things are become new" (2 Cor. 5:17). "For in Christ Jesus neither circumcision availeth any thing, nor uncircumcision, but a new creature" (Gal. 6:15). Much is to be expected of the children of God in the way of a strong Christian character. "Put on the new man, which after God is created in righteousness and true holiness" (Eph. 4:24).

"Dearly beloved, I beseech you as strangers and pilgrims, abstain from fleshly lusts, which war against the soul" (1 Peter 2:11). As citizens of the heavenly kingdom we are, as strangers and pilgrims, never to feel too much at home in this world; this is only a proving ground for our eternal home. According to Peter, the penitent believers in Christ make up a "holy nation" (1 Peter 2:9).

The standards for citizenship in the kingdom are high. Jesus said, "Except your righteousness shall exceed the righteousness of the scribes and Pharisees, ye shall in no case enter into the kingdom of heaven" (Matt. 5:20). Since man really has no righteousness of his own, the only true righteousness and that which is acceptable unto God is in Christ. "If ye know that he is righteous, ye know that every one that doeth righteousness is born of him" (1 John 2:29). Thus we may see that righteousness will help to identify us as citizens of the kingdom.

Peter in his epistle gives some description of the character of the citizens of the kingdom of God when he calls the kingdom citizens "an holy nation, a peculiar people" (1 Peter 2:9). "Holiness" is not a word for the citizens of the kingdom to shun. The character of God's people should be holy, pure, and clean. "And every man that hath this hope in him purifieth himself, even as he is pure" (1 John 3:3). If we are true to the Word of God, we must hold up high standards for his people. Paul admonishes the Romans as he writes, "Even so now yield your members servants to righteousness unto holiness" (Rom. 6:19).

The kingdom citizen is a spiritual being and under the leadership of the Spirit of God. "For as many as are led by the Spirit of God, they are the sons of God" (Rom. 8:14). "For they that are after the flesh do mind the things of the flesh; but they that are after the Spirit the things of the Spirit. For to be carnally minded is death; but to be spiritually minded is life and peace" (Rom. 8:5–6).

Citizens of the kingdom of God are to be characterized further by humility, simplicity, teachability, and a sense of dependence upon the Lord. "Except ye be converted, and become as little children, ye shall not enter into the kingdom of heaven" (Matt. 18:3). There is no place for false pride, worldly ambition, arrogancy, and an attitude of self-sufficiency among the citizens of the kingdom of God.

What are some of the privileges of citizenship in the kingdom of God? To fully appreciate citizenship in the kingdom of heaven one may do well to remember "the rock whence ye are hewn" and compare the privileges of kingdom citizenship with the condition of those who are unsaved and with one's own condition before being born into the kingdom of God.

The man without heavenly citizenship is living under the dominion of sin and Satan in the realms of death and darkness. He is "dead in trespasses and sins." He is without "hope, and without God in the world." "The wrath of God abideth on him," and he is walking "according to the course of this world." He is possessed with the spirit of disobedience and is "fulfilling the desires of the flesh and of the mind." Saved from such a state as this and made children of God, one is caused to marvel with John, "Behold, what manner of love the Father hath bestowed upon us, that we should be called the sons of God" (1 John 3:1).

The citizen of the kingdom of God enjoys a life of light in contrast with the old life of darkness. "But ye are a chosen generation; a royal priesthood, an holy nation, a peculiar people; that ye should shew forth the praises of him who hath called you out of darkness into his marvellous light" (1 Peter 2:9). From darkness to light is a marvelous transformation and the glorious experience of the citizens of the kingdom.

The citizens of the kingdom are also blessed as "a royal priesthood." This suggests the blessed privilege of direct access to God through our great High Priest, Jesus Christ. Some take such a circuitous route to get to God and interpose so many uncalled-for intermediaries that they reduce their status from that of a royal priesthood to the place of having almost to come by the "back door" to get the attention of God and to gain an audience with him. There are some who put the church, the ordinances of the church, the virgin Mary, the saints, the priest, and their rosary between themselves and their otherwise direct approach to God through Jesus Christ, despite the fact that Paul declares, "There is one God, and one mediator between God and men, the man Christ Jesus" (1 Tim. 2:5).

Why not take advantage of our privileges of coming directly to God through Christ as members of a "royal priesthood" and as citizens of the kingdom of heaven? In Revelation 5:10 we read that the Lord has "made us unto our God kings and priests." What an inspiration this is to the citizens of the kingdom!

One of the great privileges of being a citizen of the heavenly kingdom is to enjoy fellowship with the King. The King does not hold himself aloof from his people. He is accessible at all times. He is sensitive to the cry of the humblest believer. He is never too busy to give attention to those who approach God in his name. They are never forced to come to him as unwelcome intruders, but in simple response to his own gracious invitation of love and mercy. "Come unto me, all ye that labour and are heavy laden, and I will give you rest" (Matt. 11:28). This is typical of the attitude of Jesus toward all of us. "Him that cometh to me I will in no wise cast out" (John 6:37). No one ever comes to Jesus only to be turned away empty-handed and emptyhearted, but in approaching him humbly and trustingly, the person will always be satisfied.

The King is one who wants intimate association with his followers. He regards us neither as his slaves nor as his servants, but rather as his intimate friends. "Henceforth I call you not servants; for the servant knoweth not what his lord doeth: but I have called you friends; for all things that I have heard of my Father I have made known unto you" (John 15:15). Not only are we friends of the King, but we are a part of the royal family of the King, with family relationships and privileges. Jesus said, "Whosoever shall do the will of God, the same is my brother, and my sister, and mother" (Mark 3:35). The kingdom citizen has been elevated to a place of fellowship with the King, which includes walking by his side, communing with him, and entering the holy of holies with him.

Another privilege of kingdom citizenship is in the quality of the fellow citizens—"Fellowcitizens with the saints, and of the household of God" (Eph. 2:19). The traveling companions are most desirable. The relationship is on a fraternal basis. "All ye are brethren" (Matt. 23:8).

The privileges in kingdom citizenship carry with them corresponding responsibilities. One cannot be a child of the King and insist upon living like the devil. Many times there are professing Christians who complain and lament over conditions in the world and heave apathetic sighs about the world's going to the devil. The fact remains, however, that it was never intended in the plan of God for the devil's people to have any ability or responsibility in making the world better or in saving the world from chaos. The world, as such, will never be saved. The world, in the Scriptures, is the very symbol of that which is carnal and materialistic —not Christlike! While the world, as such, may never be saved, God is at work saving penitent, trusting souls out of the world. Any changes in people and any changes in conditions pertaining to light shining in darkness, the crooked being made straight, and the corrupt being purified is related to the responsibility of God's children, who shine as lights "in the midst of a crooked and perverse nation."

God does not place the responsibility upon any except his own children. He says, "If my people, which are called by my name, shall humble themselves, and pray, and seek my face, and turn from their wicked ways; then will I hear from heaven, and will forgive their sin, and will heal their land" (2 Chron. 7:14). What a difference would be made in the world if God's people were as consistent in serving him as the devil's subjects are in serving their master!

Jesus referred to his disciples as "the salt of the earth." Good salt has qualities for cleansing, healing, preserving, and making more palatable. Christian people are blessed with such qualities, and how unbearable and corrupt this old world would be were it not for the very presence of God's people! It would surely collapse of its own corruptness were it not for the preserving presence of the people of God. Who, even among lost people, would deliberately choose to live in the perils of a place where there were no people of God?

Jesus said to his disciples, "Ye are the light of the world," and how dark this old world would be if all of God's people should be removed! As it is, the darkness sometimes is very depressing, and yet we can hardly conceive of such darkness as there would be were it not for the presence of God's people, who are to function as shining lights and who are to "walk as children of the light."

The godly life is the responsibility of every citizen of the kingdom of God. They are called upon to "live soberly, righteously, and godly, in this present world" (Titus 2:12). The emphasis to be made here is that even though they are children of God, they are still living in the same world in which they lived before becoming citizens of his kingdom. They are *in* the world, but they are not *of* the world. When Jesus said to his Heavenly Father, "I have manifested thy name unto the men which thou gavest me out of the world" (John 17:6), he was not suggesting that these persons should go into seclusion in some monastery, or that they should become hermits, or that they should be cut off from association with the world as hothouse plants. In the same prayer he added, "I pray not that thou shouldest take them out of the world, but that thou shouldest keep them from the evil" (John 17:15). Their responsibility is to be rightly related to the world of affairs without becoming contaminated with the world.

Every kingdom citizen has the responsibility of loyalty to King Jesus. To be a good citizen of the kingdom of God, one must make a complete break with sin, Satan, and self. If Christ is to be the King, then loyalties to the world, the flesh, and the devil must give way to loyalties to him. The loyalty of the citizens of the kingdom is an important, practical, and timely consideration. Loyalty to the King and the kingdom is one of the real evidences of our being citizens of the kingdom. Consistent loyalty requires everyday loyalty.

A loyal subject of the kingdom is no hireling. His loyalty is not something resulting from a bribe. He is not serving for wages or rewards. He will be equally loyal in prosperity and in adversity, without regard for personal gains and losses. Jesus said, "He that is an hireling, and not the shepherd, whose own the sheep are not, seeth the wolf coming, and leaveth the sheep, and fleeth: and the wolf catcheth them, and scattereth the sheep" (John 10:12). Loyalty under the fiery tests of persecution was the obvious and convincing type of citizenship in the kingdom of the apostle Paul. His testimony was, "I know both how to be abased, and I know how to abound: every where and in all things I am instructed both to be full and to be hungry, both to abound and to suffer need" (Phil. 4:12).

All the interests of the kingdom of God must originate in Christ, emanate and radiate from Christ, be crystallized and converge upon Christ. He is the controlling power of his kingdom. He is the co-ordinating and integrating force of his kingdom. "By him all things consist [hold together]," implying that apart from the cohesive powers that bind us together and unto him in the kingdom, we as individuals would disintegrate and go to pieces in confusion. His mighty presence and directing power are needed.

Citizens of the kingdom owe their unreserved allegiance to Christ. Such loyalty must be motivated by love. "For the love of Christ constraineth us" (2 Cor. 5:14). Loyalty motivated by love expresses itself in cheerful obedience. "For this is the love of God, that we keep his commandments: and his commandments are not grievous" (1 John 5:3). Napoleon reportedly said, "Great empires are founded by men upon force—Jesus alone founded his empire upon love, and this very day millions would die for him." Loyal citizens of the kingdom are produced only in proportion as they honor the pre-eminence of Christ.

Loyalty in the kingdom of God calls for a life of faithful service. God's people are to be "zealous of good works" (Titus 2:14). This means anxious, willing, and enthusiastic about the work of the Lord. This presents quite a contrast to the old man in the barbershop who was greeted one morning with the inquiry, "How are you today?" to which he replied, "I eat well, sleep well, look well, and feel well, but I have no desire for work." If God's people are as well off spiritually as this old man thought he was physically, they will have a desire to work. "Wherefore, receiving a kingdom that cannot be shaken, let us have grace, whereby we may offer service well-pleasing to God with reverence and awe" (Heb. 12:28, ASV).

The kingdom citizen has the responsibility for growth. The

citizen of the kingdom of God never reaches his maximum for Christ while he is here in this world. There is always need for growth and development and for the unfolding processes of a child of God who is growing "in grace, and in the knowledge of our Lord and Saviour Jesus Christ."

All of God's plans and purposes are geared to a progressive scale. No one expects or requires maturity at birth. No one expects or requires maximum at the beginning. For every citizen of the kingdom there is always need and room for additional growth and development. We are not born full grown. We are born with growing potentialities. We are born with growing opportunities. Paul never reached the place where he could not see a challenge for still reaching for the unattained. "Brethren, I count not myself to have apprehended: but this one thing I do, forgetting those things which are behind, and reaching forth unto those things which are before, I press toward the mark for the prize of the high calling of God in Christ Jesus" (Phil. 3:13–14).

God's children have a secure place in a secure kingdom. The citizens of the kingdom of God enjoy a security that far surpasses anything among the kingdoms of this world. Great kingdoms of men like the Roman Empire have risen only to fall, and the subjects have often suffered utter defeat. In our generation men have been citizens of countries that have fallen into the dust of defeat. Citizenship in the kingdom of heaven is as abiding as the kingdom itself, which is eternal and indestructible. The credentials for citizenship in this kingdom are indestructible. They are credentials which the world cannot give and the world cannot take away. The citizen of the kingdom of God is fortified against the wiles of the devil, who can never deprive him of his citizenship title and privileges.

The saving experience with Jesus Christ which transplants one from the kingdom of the world into the kingdom of God is a permanent transaction. Our Lord, who is the King of his kingdom, does not operate in transitory circles. He moves and functions in the realm of the eternal. His investments, his holdings, and his achievements are of enduring quality. Christ has constantly placed emphasis upon eternal or everlasting life. In his kingdom we are not the recipients of, or the participants in, that which is here today and gone tomorrow. The King of our kingdom, Jesus, is mightier than all of the adversaries of the citizens of the kingdom. He is no king in exile, and we are no orphaned children.

The citizens of the kingdom of God have been delivered from the penalty of sin. They are now being delivered from the power of sin. One glad day they will be delivered from the presence of sin. However, only when this mortal shall become immortal, the earthly becomes the heavenly, and the corruptible becomes the incorruptible shall the latter take place. Of every true citizen of his kingdom it may well be said, "Greater is he that is in you, than he that is in the world" (1 John 4:4), and ". . . he which hath begun a good work in you will perform it until the day of Jesus Christ" (Phil. 1:6). Citizens of the kingdom enjoy the preserving power of him who ever protects his own. "They shall never perish, neither shall any man pluck them out of my hand" (John 10:28).

The King is a conquering King, in keeping with the purposes of his first advent into the world. "For this purpose the Son of God was manifested, that he might destroy the works of the devil" (1 John 3:8). He does not have to wait until he comes the second time "conquering, and to conquer" as the "King of kings, and Lord of lords," but, rather, in the days in which we live he is willing to make bare his mighty arms in our behalf and against the forces of evil if we will only rely upon him and refrain from isolating ourselves from him and undertaking so much in our own strength.

There is further security taught in the reference to his people as a "peculiar people" (1 Peter 2:9). This suggests not only that God's people are set apart as a different type of people from those in the world of sin, but the thought of their being God's treasure, his own possession, is involved here. He will protect his treasures inasmuch as he has made a great investment in us; and he loves and cherishes us and keeps us safely from murderers, thieves, and robbers.

The citizens of his kingdom have their names enrolled in heaven, where Satan cannot get to the records to erase or deface them. While the writer to the Hebrews is anticipating the assembly in heaven, he at the same time gives us assurance of the heavenly record now. "To the general assembly and church of the firstborn, which are written in heaven" (Heb. 12:23).

The citizens of the kingdom of heaven have an inheritance that is secure. It can never be lost or destroyed. It is well protected and well preserved. In the living hope which we have from God through the resurrection of Jesus Christ from the dead he hath begotten us "to an inheritance incorruptible, and undefiled, and that fadeth not away, reserved in heaven for you, Who are kept by the power of God through faith unto salvation ready to be revealed in the last time" (1 Peter 1:4–5). We shall one day come into our full inheritance, which is as sure as that of Jesus Christ himself, because we are "joint-heirs" with him; and before God can disinherit his redeemed children, he would have to disinherit his own and only begotten Son.

The security of the kingdom citizen may further be seen in the great doctrines of the plan of salvation, which become experiences of grace in the lives of God's redeemed children. The kingdom citizen is justified in the sight of God, "being justified freely by his grace through the redemption that is in Christ Jesus" (Rom. 3:24). "Therefore being justified by faith, we have peace with God through our Lord Jesus Christ" (Rom. 5:1).

The kingdom citizen also has been adopted into the family of God, which gives an added guarantee of his security and of his inheritance. The adopted child cannot be disinherited, even by the laws of the land. "For ye have not received the spirit of bondage again to fear; but ye have received the Spirit of adoption, whereby we cry, Abba, Father" (Rom. 8:15). The "Abba, Father" is an endearing term, and he speaks the endearment of the Father to the son and of the son to the Father with intimate ties of affection.

The kingdom of this world may be blasted to pieces in a nuclear war, but the citizenship in the kingdom of God stands sure. Men might be carried away as captives in strange lands and lose all connection with the land of their nativity in this world, but such cannot destroy the citizenship in God's unshakable kingdom. The thrones of men may totter, but their King shall never be dethroned, and they shall always be privileged to "come boldly unto the throne of grace, . . . obtain mercy, and find grace to help in time of need" (Heb. 4:16).

Victorious living should characterize the lives of the kingdom citizens. They may live victoriously over Satan, sin, self, ignorance, enemies, and death itself. Jesus gives such encouragement for victorious living when he says, "Be of good cheer; I have overcome the world" (John 16:33). There is no place among the citizens of the kingdom for pessimism or a spirit of gloomy defeat. God's people may possess a spirit of enthusiastic optimism at all times.

Much of the New Testament was written in a day when the citizens of the kingdom were living under the heavy and severe hand of persecution, when men "loved not their lives unto the death" and were "faithful unto death." In the midst of much hostility to the cause of Christ and to his followers the triumphant notes were sounded many times and unsurpassed courage was demonstrated in the strength of the triumphant Lord and King enthroned in their hearts. What a testimony is this from the apostles who rejoiced "that they were counted worthy to suffer shame for his name" (Acts 5:41).

These early citizens of the kingdom lived triumphantly and died victoriously. The apostle Paul, confronted with bonds and afflictions, maintained his position in Christ unwaveringly as he declared, "But none of these things move me, neither count I my life dear unto myself, so that I might finish my course with joy, and the ministry, which I have received of the Lord Jesus, to testify the gospel of the grace of God" (Acts 20:24). It was a note of confident and victorious living when the apostle Paul concluded, "If God be for us, who can be against us?" (Rom. 8:31). The kingdom man on a conquest for Christ the King could with abiding assurance testify that "in all these things we are more than conquerors through him that loved us" (Rom. 8:37).

The citizen of the kingdom was living above his sufferings when he wrote, "For I reckon that the sufferings of this present time are not worthy to be compared with the glory which shall be revealed in us" (Rom. 8:18). The citizen of the kingdom was triumphing with the eternal over the transient in the very midst of affliction when he wrote, "For our light affliction, which is but for a moment, worketh for us a far more exceeding and eternal weight of glory" (2 Cor. 4:17). The kingdom citizen has such faith and vision and his outlook is so bright that he can look beyond death, hell, and the grave with a complete sense of victory and with gratitude to God. "But thanks be to God, which giveth us the victory through our Lord Jesus Christ" (1 Cor. 15:57).

The citizen of the kingdom of heaven has many sweet and inspiring aspirations and anticipations. "Our citizenship is in heaven; whence also we wait for a Saviour, the Lord Jesus Christ" (Phil. 3:20, ASV). The kingdom citizen is expecting, longing for, and waiting for the return of the Lord. To him the return of the Lord is the realization of, and the consummation of, that blessed hope about which Paul wrote to Titus, "Looking for that blessed hope, and the glorious appearing of the great God and our Saviour Jesus Christ" (Titus 2:13).

The kingdom citizen is anticipating his eternal heavenly home that is infinitely better than all that this world can afford; he is never going to be too well satisfied with, or bound to, this world. "They desire a better country, that is, an heavenly" (Heb. 11:16). While here, "We walk by faith, not by sight" (2 Cor. 5:7).

The preparation of the kingdom citizen will be aimed Godward and heavenward. He will have no difficulty heeding the admonition of Christ when he said, "But lay up for yourselves treasures in heaven, where neither moth nor rust doth corrupt, and where thieves do not break through nor steal" (Matt. 6:20). It is the anticipation of being like Jesus. "Beloved, now are we the sons of God, and it doth not yet appear what we shall be: but we know that, when he shall appear, we shall be like him; for we shall see him as he is" (1 John 3:2).

Six

Membership in the Church

A RE YOU A CHRISTIAN?" the witness for Christ asked the unsaved man. He replied, "I belong to the church." The witness an-
swered, "So do the pews belong to the church, along with the
other church furnishings."

Church membership is no guarantee of salvation. One may
possess church membership without possession of Christ. Pos-
sessing Christ and being a qualified member of a New Testament
church means more than membership in all of the clubs, lodges,
fraternities, associations, and organizations among men. Church
membership is related to the past, present, and future of one's
life. Church membership presupposes regeneration and baptism;
it anticipates continued opportunities for worship and service;
and it carries with it certain inescapable current responsibilities.

Church membership must be related to kingdom membership.
Church membership presupposes kingdom citizenship, and kingdom citizenship should anticipate church membership. One of the
purposes of this chapter is to present the significance of church
membership as the sequel to kingdom citizenship. No one is
going to be a good citizen of the kingdom without church membership. Obtaining or attaining church membership is the consideration at this point. It is one thing, however, to attain or ob-

tain church membership, and another thing to maintain church membership.

Who is a member of the church? This is a pertinent question. The answer, in the light of certain scriptural requirements and standards, may indicate that not all are members of the church who claim to be or who think that they are.

One might well ask the person who claims to be a church member after years of absenteeism, inactivity, and nonresident membership: "What makes you think that you are still a member of the church?" These are timely questions and call for prayerful study and constructive answers. People do not inherit membership in a church like membership in a family or citizenship in a country. People do not become members of New Testament churches by proxy, through simply having the parents to take care of it while the children are in their early infancy.

Membership in the New Testament *ekklēsia* was, and is, different from membership in the Hebrew or the Greek *ekklēsia*. The terms for admission make them quite different. No one is a fit subject for baptism and church membership who has not been born again. The spiritual birth is into the kingdom and family of God. No one is considered a full-fledged member of any church without baptism in some form, according to the beliefs and teachings of the particular group, but regeneration must precede water baptism.

It has been pointed out that kingdom membership depends upon a birth, and membership in the New Testament church depends upon a burial. Baptism as a burial cannot be the same thing in act, mode, design, or achievement as a birth. The question of how one becomes a member of a New Testament church is a timely one. Our statements may be familiarly trite to some; yet, our treatise would be incomplete without some specific references in this connection.

In considering church membership, the one who is desirous of becoming affiliated with the church must first of all give evidence of having repented of sins and give a testimony or a profession of saving faith in Jesus Christ. Evidence must be given of kingdom citizenship. This ought to be a public profession of faith in Christ.

At this point some consideration should be given to the reception of new church members. Those who contend that the church and the kingdom are identical do not understand the purpose of voting upon new church members. Issue is taken on the assumption that people are being voted into the kingdom of God. The vote of the church upon new members has nothing to do with kingdom membership, other than presupposing membership in the kingdom as a requirement for the applicant's membership in the church. Perhaps one of the reasons that we may have so many unsaved people in our churches is the slack and shallow ways in which they are received. The man who said that the devil could dress up and join the majority of our churches any Sunday morning was not too far wrong.

Some churches have a waiting period, during which new converts are carefully and prayerfully interviewed by capable committees before they are finally recommended for church membership. When a new convert presents himself for membership upon public profession of faith in Christ, the church, functioning as a democratic body, has the privilege either to receive or reject the individual, according to the discretion of the particular church. The affirmative vote is an expression of confidence in the genuine experience of grace professed by the applicant for church affiliation. It is an expression of confidence in the sincerity and worthiness of the motives of the convert. It is an invitation to him to enjoy fellowship in the church with others of like faith, after immersion as authorized by the church, which serves as the custodian of the ordinances of baptism and the Lord's Supper.

If time does not permit consideration of the church covenant at the point of the reception of a candidate for baptism and church membership, the pastor and the new member committee or the church cabinet would do well to set a time to meet the one in question for consultation and instruction and to see if that individual is willing to subscribe to the principles of the church covenant, and to place a copy of the same in his hands if such has not previously been done.

Having dealt briefly with the question of obtaining church membership, let us now continue with the matter of maintaining church membership. Here we will find many fences that need mending and much propping up to be done on the leaning side.

"I am a Baptist," said the sixty-five-year-old man to the census taker in the city. "Is your membership in this community?" "No, my membership is in a country church in west Tennessee." "How long has it been since you left the community where your church membership is?" "Almost fifty years," was the reply.

Further inquiry revealed that this man's wife was not a member of any church and that neither of them had attended church anywhere for many years. The man proved to be very hostile toward churches and Christian people in general. It developed that his reputation in the community was one of drinking heavily. He cursed his wife loudly, promiscuously, and profusely. Should he decide to join a church in the community by letter, his letter might read that he was in full fellowship. He probably is still carried on a church roll where nobody remembers who he is and where nobody knows or cares very much where he has gone.

This illustration might be repeated many times over in the territory of the Southern Baptist Convention. There is no ready-made, "fit-all" solution, but sometimes we may need to shock some of these people into the realization that perhaps in the sight of God their names' being on the church roll means absolutely nothing, even though they would like for their obituary column to mention their church affiliation. It is one thing to become a member of the church, and it is another thing to *maintain* membership in the church. The writer firmly believes that all of our churches are carrying the names of many persons on their church rolls who, strictly speaking, have forfeited their right to be classified as church members.

There are about two million Southern Baptists who are living in one place with their church membership in some other place. They are described as absentee, or nonresident, members. These figures are becoming alarming to all of us, because they represent people who are precious in God's sight and to whom our churches have a definite responsibility for a spiritual ministry. With such staggering numbers of the unenlisted, our task of enlistment is a gigantic one and our failures in conserving the results of evangelism should put us all to shame.

There are two truths about churches which are set forth clearly and repeatedly in the New Testament. One is that the church is a called-out assembly of believers in Christ. The other is that the church is a fellowship of believers in Christ.

Much emphasis is placed upon both of these characteristics. God's plan for his people through the churches is for them to assemble at regular times, at appointed places, for the worship of God and for their mutual edification through fellowship with one another in Christ. When there was a slackness in the assembling together, the writer to the Hebrews issued a warning admonition, in which he said, "Not forsaking the assembling of ourselves together, as the manner of some is" (Heb. 10:25).

Paul made much of the fellowship as he wrote to the Galatians: "And when James, Cephas, and John, who seemed to be pillars, perceived the grace that was given unto me, they gave to me and Barnabas the right hands of fellowship" (Gal. 2:9). It was said of the early church in Jerusalem, "And they continued stedfastly in the apostles' doctrine and fellowship, and in breaking of bread, and in prayers" (Acts 2:42). Paul had a prayerful concern for the Philippians with reference to their fellowship in the gospel.

Now, if attendance and fellowship are such vital components of church membership, how can there be either of them among those who are nonresident members or among those who seldom, if ever, attend their church that is nearby?

One might raise the question of the propriety of granting letters of dismissal for someone who finally has united with another church of like faith and order and stating on the letter that the individual was in full fellowship when they have not attended a service in ten years. What kind of a fellowship is it among people who never see each other, never worship together, never meet together, and never do anything together in the Lord's service? What kind of an assembly can be had with people who do not assemble? How can one be a member of the assembly without assembling or without ever attending?

If we let the word "church"—*ekklēsia*—mean what it has meant in the Greek language through the years, we may be compelled to inform a number of people on our church rolls that their membership has expired through failure to assemble and through a lack of fellowship. The same principle might apply to the membership in a convention. How long should or could one be considered a member of a convention without ever convening?

What then is the meaning of church membership? From a study of the New Testament churches we may reach a number of interrelated conclusions.

Church membership certainly means togetherness with God's people. The figure of speech in which the church is likened unto a building would illustrate this fact—"all the building fitly framed together" (Eph. 2:21). The binding cords of love also produce and indicate this togetherness among the members of the church. "Being knit together in love" (Col. 2:2) is the description that Paul again gives of the church family.

Church members are the appealed-to ones in having been among the "called out" ones; the apart ones, separated from the world of sin; the added ones, added to the church daily as saved; the associated ones, together in worship, fellowship, service; the assembled ones, coming together for a particular meeting; the assigned ones, carrying on under a divine commission; the accepted ones, accepted in the beloved; and the active ones, engaging in spiritual exercises.

The fellowship in the church may be interpreted and applied, to some extent, by the employment of some other words, including lordship, partnership, stewardship, and friendship.

A true fellowship of baptized believers in Christ must be founded upon, and centered in, the lordship of Jesus Christ. It is from him that all receive their commission as the same authoritative source. One supreme authority must be recognized, accepted, and honored in order for all to be unified, harmonized, and moving in the same direction. If this is not true, the fellowship may be broken by overly ambitious members who vie with one another for pre-eminence. John, in his third epistle, refers to Diotrephes as a character of the type to break the fellowship. John said, "I wrote unto the church: but Diotrephes, who loveth to have the preeminence among them, receiveth us not" (3 John 9). The Lord Jesus Christ is the one to whom all are mutually and equally subject. When he is so respected, a harmonious and lovely fellowship will exist in the church. All personal and petty differences among church members will be dissolved when the lordship of Christ becomes a reality in the church. He alone deserves the place of pre-eminence as the incomparable Christ.

The element of a partnership is to be found in the true fellowship of the baptized believers in Christ. This partnership-fellowship principle has its source in the common investment of the redeeming death of Christ on the cross in those who constitute the fellowship and who have established the partnership. This common investment of the partnership brings to our attention the common ownership. All of the baptized believers, who are voluntarily associated together for the purpose of propagating the gospel of Christ, belong to the same Lord and are equally dependent upon and responsible to him. Paul wrote the Corinthians, "All are yours; and ye are Christ's; and Christ is God's" (1 Cor. 3: 22–23).

In the partnership among fellow Christians the fact of interdependence among the members must be accepted; they all need each other for normal and fruitful functioning. As an illustration of the need for a recognition of interdependence, Paul said, "The eye cannot say unto the hand, I have no need of thee: nor again the head to the feet, I have no need of thee" (1 Cor. 12:21). In this fellowship-partnership relationship we are taught to "bear . . . one another's burdens, and so fufil the law of Christ" (Gal. 6:2). "We then that are strong ought to bear the infirmities of the weak" (Rom. 15:1).

In this idea of the fellowship-partnership among fellow church members, they may be privileged to share in certain blessings that are common to all of them. The spiritual prosperity of the

church should be shared by every member. Joy over the salvation of the lost is something to be shared by every member.
Spiritual victories are to be shared by all.

All of the members of the fellowship-partnership should indi-
vidually and collectively accept the responsibilities incumbent
upon the true servants of Jesus Christ. No undue burdens should
ever be placed upon the faithful few while many others totally
escape commitments and responsibilities for the welfare and the
program of the church. Shared responsibilities develop maturer
Christians and make for a stronger church.

A genuine fellowship of baptized believers in Christ, who are
associated together in the Lord's work, will create true friendships
among these same people. The fellowship can be strengthened or
weakened by the friendship, or lack of it, among the church
members. It will be a weak fellowship where the members see
each other, greet each other, and know each other only within
the church building. Friendship ties that carry over through the
week and that overshadow all class and social levels and lines
will strengthen the spiritual fellowship of the church. Members
who are ostracized through the week from the social lives of their
fellow members will not enjoy the best fellowship at the church
on Sunday. Members who are ignored through the week will not
respond readily to a Sunday smile and handshake. Cliques and
clans of friends of the same social level and preference in a church
can carry such to an extreme. They create a "left out" feeling in
other members. This produces irreparable damage to the fellowship of the church.

Many new members do not enjoy the fellowship of the church
because they sense that those who have been in the church
through the years are rather clannish. They become frustrated in
their efforts to gain recognition. A relationship of friendliness is
a blessed fellowship. A fellowship of friendship in mutual helpfulness is much to be desired when there are those who are sick,
in sorrow, in distress, or in need of any kind. The church covenant teaches us to look after one another in many kinds of needs.
There is many a lonely church member who feels neglected, for-

gotten, and forsaken in the midst of affliction, and they are starving for a little bit of Christian love and sympathy.

The writer did the preaching in a series of revival services in a rural church. One of the older brethren was sick and unable to harvest his crop. At the close of one of the evening services the faithful pastor for twenty-three years said, "Men, meet me at Brother Jones' in the morning bright and early; we are going to harvest his crop." And they did. Such a spirit of brotherly love and friendly helpfulness fulfils the law of Christ. It is lacking in too many churches.

A true fellowship will express itself in a worthy and faithful stewardship. In a genuine fellowship of baptized believers in Christ members should not hold on to the Lord's money as though it were theirs. Church members should not waste money upon themselves and depend upon fellow members to do all of the sacrificing and denying of themselves in order to promote the work of the Lord. In the larger stewardship the fellowship must be expressed in the joining of hands and hearts as the custodians of the gospel, of the ordinances, of the offerings, of the building and grounds, and of all that the church may undertake, according to divine command and guidance.

There are many responsibilities associated with church membership. Let us consider briefly the responsibilities of consecration, soul-winning, stewardship, and attendance, along with some blessings and rewards.

The professing Christian and church member has the responsibility of living a life that is separate from the world of sin, so far as familiarity and indulgence are concerned. Paul appealed to the Corinthians for such a life when he wrote, "Wherefore come out from among them, and be ye separate, saith the Lord, and touch not the unclean thing; and I will receive you . . ." (2 Cor. 6:17). The life of the Christian and faithful church member must be lived with an eye single to God's glory. "Whether therefore ye eat, or drink, or whatsoever ye do, do all to the glory of God" (1 Cor. 10:31).

Those who are saved have been saved to serve. Paul wrote the

Ephesians, "For we are his workmanship, created in Christ Jesus unto good works, which God hath before ordained that we should walk in them" (Eph. 2:10). Church membership for the child of God enhances the opportunities for Christian service and increases the responsibility for Christian service.

It is the duty of every child of God, and especially those who are affiliated with the churches, to be a witness for Christ. God never intended to place all of the responsibility for soul-winning upon the pastors and evangelists or upon the paid staff of the church. He never intended to overload a few of the faithful church members while the overwhelming majority relax amid their indolent complacency. He never planned for one to do all of another's Christian service any more than he intended for one to be saved for another, for one to eat for another, or for one to answer for another at the judgment bar of God.

It has often been said that "the first cry of a newborn soul is another soul." "It is the duty of every child of God to seek constantly to win the lost to Christ by personal effort and by all other methods sanctioned by the gospel of Christ." This quotation is taken from the tract *The Baptist Faith and Message.* In a day of full-time pastors and enlarged church staffs all too few of the members of the churches take the business of soul-winning seriously. So many salve their consciences with material contributions and neglect to witness personally for Christ on the ground that they are helping to pay someone else to do it.

All of life is a stewardship. As children of God, we are his by creation, by redemption, and by birth or regeneration. He has a rightful claim upon us by virtue of the investment that he has made in us through the supreme sacrifice of his only begotten Son on the cross. Indeed, we are not our own, having been bought with a price, according to Paul in 1 Corinthians 6:19–20. We are to honor God with every area of life, with every fiber of our being, and with all with which we have to do materially and otherwise.

Membership in the church affords the individual a wonderful opportunity, not only for the development of God-given talents, but also for the utilization of talents in kingdom service and for God's glory. The writer has never discovered any type of Christian service that really honors God and advances his kingdom but what the church is supposed to encourage, sponsor, and promote it. A well-organized, virile church will include in its program all kinds of Christian service.

Occasionally there are church members who insist upon giving the tithe to scattered causes outside the church, in conflict with the Bible plan of tithes and offerings being given through the church. The writer, as a pastor, challenges the members at the time the annual budget is being prepared to assist in seeing that every phase of the ministry of our Lord is included in the budget and that every New Testament cause has a place. The members are reminded that if they are now supporting worthy causes outside the church with their money to please call such to the attention of the budget committee. Such individuals have been invited to appear before the budget committee, and in almost every instance it has been proved that the church was already supporting in a far more fruitful way the same type of ministry that had attracted certain members of the church. In addition to this fact, it has been shown that causes supported by the churches are under church control and denominational control and are supervised in such a way that every contributing or participating church has a voice in what is done with the money.

In the stewardship of material possessions the members of our churches should be taught that the tithe is the minimum, not from a legalistic point of view, but from hearts of genuine love and gratitude unto him who has given us life and all that sustains and enriches life, who has given for us and to us his own life. The tithe is not something to be exacted from God's people by enforcement of law, but it is inspired by the stronger appeals of grace. If the Jews under the law were required to give a tithe back to God, those under grace should not expect to give less and should be willing to give more.

The principle of stewardship may be applied from the simple teaching that "for unto whomsoever much is given, of him shall be much required" (Luke 12:48). God has graciously given his all to us in his Son Jesus, and we who are the recipients and beneficiaries of his grace should dedicate our all unto him through the high motives of love in contrast with the low motives of fear, force, and formalism.

The whole world should be in the prayers, vision, and compassionate concern of Christians and church members. Ours is a trusteeship and debtorship to the whole world. Paul acknowledged his debtorship and was ready to pay, with the best that was in him, through sharing the gospel with others. He said: "I am debtor both to the Greeks, and to the Barbarians; both to the wise, and to the unwise. So, as much as in me is, I am ready to preach the gospel to you that are at Rome also. For I am not ashamed of the gospel of Christ: for it is the power of God unto salvation to every one that believeth; to the Jew first, and also to the Greek" (Rom. 1:14–16). The responsibility of every Christian and church member is to be missionary in mind, missionary in word, and missionary in deed.

Then there is the responsibility of attendance in connection with church membership. God's plan of the ages has been for his people to come together at an appointed place, at an appointed hour, or on an appointed day to worship the true and living God. The plan has been devised by divine knowledge. God knows how his children need the discipline of having specific times for worship and how prone they are to be negligent. According to the knowledge that God has of the needs of his own children, he has designed the hour of worship in an assembly of his people to help meet the spiritual needs of his children and to glorify himself.

The plan of worship in the assembly has been provided and projected not only by divine knowledge but as an expression of divine love. God's love for us affords us an opportunity and the privilege of communing with him. A properly conducted worship service is a means of our lovingly responding to God's love. Love begets love, and love responds to love.

The plan of worship in the assembly has been ordered of God.

"But unto the place which the Lord your God shall choose out of all your tribes to put his name there, even unto his habitation shall ye seek, and thither thou shalt come" (Deut. 12:5). "Gather the people together, men, and women, and children, and thy stranger that is within thy gates" (Deut. 31:12). "Gather thou all the congregation together" (Lev. 8:3). "Thou shalt worship the Lord thy God, and him only shalt thou serve" (Matt. 4:10). These are timely references on the plan of God, in which he authorizes the assembly of his people for worship.

God not only gives commands which authorize the assembling of his people for worship, but he also gives instructions concerning the participation in the worship services. "Give unto the Lord the glory due unto his name: bring an offering, and come before him: worship the Lord in the beauty of holiness" (1 Chron. 16:29). "God is a Spirit: and they that worship him must worship him in spirit and in truth" (John 4:24). God uses human instrumentality in summoning his people to assemble for worship. Every member of the church has some responsibility in promoting attendance upon the worship services. One of the perils and tragedies that is being enacted every Lord's Day in many of our churches is not simply the failure of the people to assemble at God's house, but also the number of people who come to Sunday school and leave before the worship service. They may ease their consciences to some extent by being in a Sunday school class for a few minutes—which within itself is both desirable and commendable—but it was never intended that such should take the place of the assembly for worship. "O come, let us worship and bow down: let us kneel before the Lord our maker" (Psalm 95:6). "And Hezekiah sent to all Israel and Judah, and wrote letters also to Ephraim and Manasseh, that they should come to the house of the Lord at Jerusalem, to keep the passover unto the Lord God of Israel" (2 Chron. 30:1).

God's blessings are upon those who worship him in his house and who praise him and serve him at the appointed place. "Blessed are they that dwell in thy house: they will be still praising thee" (Psalm 84:4). A joyous worship hour in God's house is a foretaste of heaven and may even symbolize the activities in the heavenly home around the throne of God, where there shall be ceaseless praises unto him and where we will be ever at home with him.

The worship service in a New Testament church is far different from that of the ancient Jews, who brought their sacrifices to the altar. Christ is the ever adequate and abiding sacrifice. He has tasted death for every man. "But we see Jesus, who was made a little lower than the angels for the suffering of death, crowned with glory and honour; that he by the grace of God should taste death for every man" (Heb. 2:9). "Who needeth not daily, as those high priests, to offer up sacrifice, first for his own sins, and then for the people's: for this he did once, when he offered up himself" (Heb. 7:27).

Our Lord has given us a worthy example in going to God's house on God's Day for the reading of the Scriptures, for an interpretation and application of the same, and to pay homage unto God. When he came into Nazareth, which was his boyhood home, we are told that "as his custom was, he went into the synagogue on the sabbath day, and stood up for to read" (Luke 4:16).

Shortly after the crucifixion and resurrection of Christ, we read about how the two who had met the resurrected Christ on the road to Emmaus found "the eleven gathered together, and them that were with them" (Luke 24:33). The pattern and practice of the Christ-instructed early church in Jerusalem was that of assembling themselves together, and it was into such an assembly of prayer and expectancy that the Holy Spirit descended in mighty power, as the Lord had promised. "And when the day of Pentecost was fully come, they were all with one accord in one place" (Acts 2:1). In the midst of this soul-winning revival, we discover that the new converts who soon were baptized and added to the church also found their places in the assembly. "And all that believed were together" (Acts 2:44). Upon returning from one of his missionary journeys, the apostle Paul and Barnabas had the members of the church come together. "And when they were come, and had gathered the church together, they rehearsed all that God had done with them, and how he had opened the door of faith unto the Gentiles" (Acts 14:27). There seemed to be no problem in getting missionary-minded church members to assemble together for a missionary message.

The writer of the seventy-third Psalm became so discouraged and depressed that it was almost unbearable for him, and he did not get any relief or find any solution until he went into God's house; or, as we would say today, until he went back to church. His own words were, "Until I went into the sanctuary of God; then understood I their end" (Psalm 73:17). He had a new outlook, a renewed hope, and a convincing testimony after his return to God's house. This becomes the real climax to the psalm: "But it is good for me to draw near to God: I have put my trust in the Lord God, that I may declare all thy works" (Psalm 73:28). Many a problem may be solved in turning worshipfully to God's house. When threatened by the Assyrians, King Hezekiah "rent his clothes, and covered himself with sackcloth, and went into the house of the Lord" (Isa. 37:1).

Just as there are many blessings to be found through church attendance, there are also many blessings lost through absenteeism. One of the things that stand out in what we know about Thomas in the New Testament is that he was a doubting absentee. "But Thomas, one of the twelve, called Didymus, was not with them when Jesus came" (John 20:24). Thomas demanded more proof of the risen Lord than the testimony of the other disciples. He was a doubting pessimist. He was absent from the assembly of the disciples on the Lord's Day, which was the first day of the week. His absence has never been fully explained. There must have been a shortage of interest, faith, co-operation, and courage. When Thomas was absent, Jesus came "and stood in the midst, and saith unto them, Peace be unto you" (John 20:19). Thomas thus missed the presence and the blessings of the Lord, along with the fellowship of the other disciples. On this occasion Thomas failed to share the joy, the assurance, and the testimony of the other disciples. But he profited by his mistake, and on the next Lord's Day he was present and gave his famous confession of the risen Lord as Christ presented the wounds of Calvary. Thomas responded with the words, "My Lord and my God" (John 20:28). He must have resolved not to be absent again.

Seven

Rules of the Church

AUTHORITY for faith and practice must reside in the Bible and not in the church. All of the revealed truth that God wants his people to have is found in the Bible. He has spoken with finality. There is no appeal beyond the authority of the Scriptures, and there is no power on earth that can set aside the authority of the Scriptures.

In the Roman Catholic Church the pope possesses the supreme authority, claiming power for setting aside the Word of God or adding to or taking from it. When he speaks ex cathedra, he claims an infallibility equal to that of Jesus Christ or equal to the revelation as we have it in the Bible. As a matter of fact, that church in practice has developed dogmas superseding the authority of Christ. The word of the pope becomes the law of the Roman Catholic Church, and to Roman Catholics the law of the kingdom of God, since they believe the church and the kingdom to be the same.

The traditions of men must never be allowed to become a substitute for the authority of the Word of God. Untold confusion results when the Word of God is set aside for the opinions and traditions of men. Jesus rebuked the Pharisees because they rejected the commandments of God and were "teaching for doctrines the

commandments of men" (Matt. 15:9). No church or kingdom
rules can ever be acceptable that are not based upon the teachings and principles of the Bible. The authority of the Bible is
founded upon divine inspiration; it is "God-breathed" and is quite
sufficient for every need of the church, for every member of the
church, and for the kingdom of God. "All scripture is given by inspiration of God, and is profitable for doctrine, for reproof, for cor-
rection, for instruction in righteousness: that the man of God may
be perfect, throughly furnished unto all good works" (2 Tim.
3:16–17).

Since the Scriptures speak authoritatively and adequately upon
every subject and in every area with which we must have to do in
faith and practice, there is no necessity for turning to any other
authority; and this applies to the doctrines, rules, and practices
of the churches as agents of the kingdom of God. No ecclesiastical
authority is needed to supplant or to supplement anything that is
taught in the Bible. A statement from *The Baptist Faith and
Message* is as follows:

We believe that the Holy Bible was written by men divinely inspired,
and is a perfect treasure of heavenly instruction; that it has God for
its author, salvation for its end, and truth, without any mixture of
error, for its matter; that it reveals the principles by which God will
judge us; and therefore is, and will remain to the end of the world,
the true center of Christian union, and the supreme standard by
which all human conduct, creeds and religious opinions should be
tried.[1]

By thus accepting the authority of the Bible there need be no
occasion for additional decrees from ecclesiastical circles. When
one speaks of "the rules of the church" in connection with the
kingdom of God, a comparative statement may be made, namely,
regarding "the laws of the kingdom," which is the subject of the
closing chapter of this book. The purpose of the rules of the
church should be to implement the laws of the kingdom. There

---

[1] *Op. cit.*, p. 5.

may be diversified rules in a church. Some of them may be classified as policies and others as principles. Most churches have bylaws as a guide in conducting the business of the church and in the organized functioning of the church. This is in the interest of an efficient organization.

Any time that a new church is constituted the members adopt certain articles of faith and principles by which they are willing to abide in a spiritual democracy. They may adopt them under the head of a "confession of faith," or they may adopt a set of bylaws by which they mutually consent to be governed.

A church as an autonomous body may amend the bylaws at any time to fit the growing needs and the changing conditions within its organized life in harmony with the principles of the Bible. While this is true of an efficiently functioning church, it would be inconceivable that any group could ever amend the laws of the kingdom of God. There are many methods and policies in the church that the Lord apparently left to the discretion of his children in implementing the fundamental principles of his program. Churches may have rules which are adopted and applied to business procedures and parliamentary laws which govern the transaction of business and methods of promotion. For example, churches may adopt rules concerning attendance. A few generations ago there were churches with strict rules governing that duty. Some of the smaller churches would call the roll, and three unexcused absences would result in the member's being censured; and those who were absent at a previous meeting were expected to give a reason for their absence.

The authority of the Scriptures, the relationship and responsibilities of the members to each other, to the church as a whole, to the Lord himself, and to the kingdom of God must determine the content of the rules of the church. Every church needs some rules concerning organizations, officers, their qualifications and duties. These rules will be influenced by the size and growth of the church.

Many churches have a covenant to which the members may commit themselves. There is a church covenant that is generally used by Southern Baptists. If the church covenant should be broken down into what might be regarded as the rules of the church, it could be considered from many points of view. First, the rule expressed in prerequisites to church membership should be considered. This consists of a personal experience of salvation through Jesus Christ in response to divine initiative. "Having been led, as we believe, by the Spirit of God, to receive the Lord Jesus Christ as our Saviour." An emphasis upon a regenerated church membership is always in order. The profession of one's faith in Christ logically follows the acceptance of Christ as Saviour, and therefore the words, "And on the profession of our faith," constitute a part of what may be expected of one who has been saved. Scriptural baptism in the name of the triune Godhead in obedience to our Lord's command is a prerequisite to full membership in a New Testament church, and the statement, " . . . having been baptized in the name of the Father, and of the Son, and of the Holy Ghost," should be included in the introduction to the rules of the church. The individual member of the church should be willing to enter into a solemn covenant in relation to the church, as stated in the following words of the covenant:

"We do now, in the presence of God, angels, and this assembly, most solemnly and joyfully enter into covenant with one another, as one body in Christ." The covenant becomes a very serious thing when one realizes that it is witnessed by God, angels, and men and that it is aimed at a fellowship with one another in Christ. Dependence upon the aid of the Holy Spirit for successfully living the Christian life and performing the duties of a church member should be readily acknowledged.

"We engage, therefore, by the aid of the Holy Spirit, to walk together in Christian love; to strive for the advancement of this church, in knowledge, holiness, and comfort; To promote its prosperity and spirituality; to sustain its worship, ordinances, discipline, and doctrines; To contribute cheerfully and regularly to the support of the ministry, the expenses of the church, the relief of the poor, and the spread of the gospel through all nations." The knowledge may come through active participation in a program of preaching, teaching, training, and individual study. The life of holiness may come through a consistent prayer life, a humble reliance upon the Holy Spirit, a faithful study of God's Word, an example of consecrated everyday living for the Lord, and an honest effort to follow in the footsteps of Jesus Christ. The comfort of the church may be provided through a genuine interest in erecting and maintaining an adequate building, adequate equipment, and such other facilities as may be helpful in making the members physically comfortable; but beyond this, in contributing to the comfort of the distressed, the bereaved, and the needy.

The prosperity and spirituality of the church may be promoted through material contributions, intercessory prayers, testimonies, and exhortation for mutual edification. These are opportunities and responsibilities belonging to every member of a church.

The worship services may be sustained through personal attendance, enlistment of others, reverence in God's house, prayer, and tithes and offerings for the glory of God. There are two church ordinances: baptism and the recurring ordinance of the Lord's Supper. The members of a church must realize that the church is the custodian of these ordinances and that they are to be protected and observed in accordance with the teachings of the New Testament.

The practice of discipline in a church has become almost a thing of the past. Many times offenses which involve serious violations of the laws of man and God are left unnoticed or without interest or attention in the church. One reason for this may be the fear of the "skillet calling the kettle black," or the fear that comes from those who live in "glass houses." It should be the accepted responsibility of every church member to hold up, and measure up to, high standards of Christian living.

Every church should have rules for discipline which are based upon the Scriptures, always with a desire to help both the offended and the offender. According to Matthew 18:15–17, the first step in settling a difference in the church is between the offended and the offender. If the offender fails to respond to conciliatory steps, a committee may be authorized to reason with the brethren, to establish the true cause for differences, and to bear witness to the steps and words designed for reconciliation. If this step fails, a third procedure is to have the matter brought to the attention of the church. If the offender fails to be influenced by the church, the final resort of the church is to accept a state of broken fellowship which has been provoked by the offender. "But if he neglect to hear the church, let him be unto thee as an heathen man and a publican" (Matt. 18:17). This verse does not place emphasis upon the idea of the church's excommunicating a member, but rather the church simply accepts a state of broken fellowship when a member refuses reconciliation and has, by his own attitude and acts, broken the fellowship. The broken fellowship may be better understood by the statement, "They went out from us, but they were not of us" (1 John 2:19).

It is obvious that one who is not in the kingdom of God has no business in the church. There are certain sins which Paul says will deny one a place in the kingdom of God. "Know ye not that the unrighteous shall not inherit the kingdom of God? Be not deceived: neither fornicators, nor idolaters, nor adulterers, nor effeminate, nor abusers of themselves with mankind, nor thieves, nor covetous, nor drunkards, nor revilers, nor extortioners, shall inherit the kingdom of God" (1 Cor. 6:9–10). If there are those in the church who promiscuously and impenitently commit these sins, they have no real place in the church, since apparently they have no place in the kingdom.

Much is said in the Scriptures about doctrines, the simple meaning of which is instruction in truth. The Jerusalem church was characterized by fidelity to the "apostles' doctrine." "They continued stedfastly in the apostles' doctrine and fellowship" (Acts 2:42). They were both consistent and persistent in their devotion to the doctrine.

The members of a church ought to know what they believe and why. The program of every church should include the teaching of the fundamental doctrines of God's Word. There are many unstable Christians because they are not well grounded in the doctrines of God. Paul sounded a timely warning when he wrote,

"That we henceforth be no more children, tossed to and fro, and carried about with every wind of doctrine, by the sleight of men, and cunning craftiness, whereby they lie in wait to deceive" (Eph. 4:14). The uninformed are easily swayed by false doctrines. Those who are ignorant of the doctrines become victims of many heresies.

Every church member may need helpful lessons on the stewardship of material possessions. The portion of the church covenant dealing with the church member, the church, and the stewardship of material possessions is well supported by Paul: "Every man according as he purposeth in his heart, so let him give: not grudgingly, or of necessity: for God loveth a cheerful giver" (2 Cor. 9:7). On the subject of regular giving the apostle also has this to say: "Upon the first day of the week let every one of you lay by him in store, as God hath prospered him, that there be no gatherings when I come" (1 Cor. 16:2).

The church covenant includes important principles that are applicable to the family and home: "We also engage to maintain family and secret devotions; to religiously educate our children; to seek the salvation of our kindred and acquaintances." A religion and a church membership that finds no expression in the home is sadly lacking.

A pastor had visited in a home where there was much strife and where the wife and mother had demonstrated an unchristian spirit. This was during a revival meeting series. In the course of the meeting this same woman started shouting in one of the services, whereupon the pastor gave expression to a spasmodic impulse and said, "Sit down, sister, until you have begun to practice your religion in your home." The church and the home are to be genuine allies. They should be complementary. The strongest homes make the strongest churches, and the strongest churches make the strongest homes. The church and the home should be strong allies.

One's everyday life before the world may weaken or strengthen the influence of the church in the community, and so the church may expect the members to walk circumspectly in the world. The circumspect person is one who watches for and sees all sides of an issue. *Circum* means "around" and *specio* means to "look." The circumspect person is watchful, prudent, and cautious. He will not be easily ensnared, will not be a ready victim of Satan's pitfalls, and is not readily turned aside from that which is basic to go off on tangents.

Church members are under the constant surveillance of the world, and the world sits in constant judgment over professing Christians and church members, looking for their faults, failures, and flaws, seldom evaluating properly what may be the virtues. A church member's dealings with others may determine the individual's spiritual stature in the community. "To be just in our dealings" is a reasonable requirement. There is no substitute for old-fashioned honesty. The old adage, "Honesty is the best policy," is an understatement. Honesty is more than a policy; it is a fundamental principle. Any kind of a shady business transaction will do irreparable damage to one's testimony and influence. People will forgive and forget most offenses more quickly than they will an unjust or unfair business deal, where a scheming person has defrauded an innocent one.

The attitude of a church member toward engagements is one worthy of consideration. It is so urgent that we be "faithful in our engagements." This may apply to every area of life every day of the week. Unfortunately for all of our churches, there are some who accept places of leadership and responsibilities who prove to be irregular in their attendance and who may fail at times even to call a substitute. Sunday school classes of boys and girls suffer at the hands of those who are unfaithful in their engagements to teach. Training Unions may suffer at the hands of those who fail to keep their engagements as leaders.

There are too many people who interpret "freedom of worship" to mean freedom *from* worship. Someone has suggested that in this day of the neglect of worship if some decree were suddenly issued which denied the right of public assembly for worship and nailed bars on the doors of the churches, the church grounds would scarcely contain the people who would be present the next Lord's Day to champion their right of worship in God's house according to the dictates of their own hearts.

Every church member is human enough to need a measure of self-discipline. For us to be "exemplary in our deportment" is necessary if the world is to see a distinction between those in the church and those out of the church. Much is expected of Christians and church members. Someone in the world of sin, who makes no pretensions toward the Christian life and who shows no interest in the church, may live an ungodly life and be all but ignored; but one infringement by a church member will provoke much criticism, become a stumbling block to others, and do lasting harm to the cause of Christ.

The right use of the tongue is an important part of the fellowship in a church. "To avoid all tattling, backbiting . . ." will help to keep down many a disturbance in a church. This particular point in the rules of the church, as set forth in the covenant, may well apply both to the individual's character and habits and to others in his relationships with them. Tattling and backbiting may not only reveal the character of the one indulging in such but also do serious injury to himself. Most tattling and backbiting are more harmful to the one so doing than to the ones who may be the objects of such. Gossip is a dangerous thing; and yet, it seems to be the favorite pastime of many idle church members who ought to be more interested in edifying others than in destroying them.

The control of one's self in the area of temper is urgent in maintaining good relations in a church. "To avoid . . . excessive anger" is a goal toward which every member should strive. There are people who are shortening their lives and crippling their influence through temper tantrums. The modern slang for it—"blowing the top"—is drawn from the idea of volcanic eruptions. Self-control is something that can be acquired through patient and persevering efforts. "He that is slow to anger is better than the mighty; and he that ruleth his spirit than he that taketh a city" (Prov. 16:32). Excessive anger in approaching problems will never solve them and may greatly complicate and aggravate whatever the difficulty may be. Where there is congregational church government, usually there are some members who will let their tempers "fly" unless they have their own way. Prayerful deliberation is the desirable approach to every issue.

"To abstain from the sale and use of intoxicating drinks as a beverage" is a portion of the church covenant that needs to be applied earnestly and prayerfully in our day. Perhaps the problem of selling alcoholic beverage in our day is not so common among church members as the problem of drinking it. If the truth really were known, there may be some who pose as leaders in nearly all of our churches who are violating this part of the church covenant. One does not have to be a drunkard to be in violation of the Scriptures and the church covenant, a transgressor of God's laws, and an unfit citizen of the kingdom of God. The social drinkers are guilty here. Those who drink at parties in the homes, at the clubs, and at the hotels are guilty. Those who sit quietly and sip the bottle in their own homes are guilty. The alcohol problem is one with which our churches need to deal frankly, firmly, and helpfully. A persistent program of education against the use of alcohol is needed in all of our churches. The churches have a great responsibility toward the improvement of the quality of kingdom citizens.

It is time for men of God to take a firm and uncompromising stand upon this evil that is such a menace to our homes, our churches, our schools, our nation, and to the health of the indulgers. Abraham Lincoln was right when he said, "Alcohol, as a beverage, may have many defenders, but no defense."

Sharing in the advancement of the kingdom of our Saviour is the big business of every church and of every individual member of a church. "To be zealous in our efforts to advance the kingdom of our Saviour" is one of the most challenging parts of the church covenant.

There is a disturbing complacency among church members in general. There is an appalling apathy among church members toward the advancement of God's kingdom. This is true to the extent that many who are supposed to be missionary-minded have a fatalistic philosophy that says in a negative attitude and in a practice of inactivity: "If the Lord wants to save the heathen, let him do it in his own good time and in his own good way. There is nothing I can do about it." God's people, in the power of the Holy Spirit, ought to be a zealous people. There ought to be some sanctified enthusiasm about the extension of his kingdom through witnessing to the lost and winning them to Christ. Church members are under a divine command to be missionary-minded and to be missionary in practice.

The church member's responsibility toward his fellow members should be an accepted part of church membership. "We further engage to watch over one another in brotherly love" is but a restatement of many of the teachings of the Bible on brotherly love. "He that loveth his brother abideth in the light, and there is none occasion of stumbling in him" (1 John 2:10). "We know that we have passed from death unto life, because we love the brethren" (1 John 3:14). "But whoso hath this world's good, and seeth his brother have need, and shutteth up his bowels of compassion from him, how dwelleth the love of God in him? My little children, let us not love in word, neither in tongue; but in deed and in truth" (1 John 3:17–18). "Beloved, if God so loved us, we ought also to love one another" (1 John 4:11). "And this commandment have we from him, that he who loveth God love his brother also" (1 John 4:21). While love is the royal law of the kingdom of God, it is likewise to be a functioning rule of the church. The business of the church is to apply this significant law of the kingdom.

Church members must recognize an interdependence. A dependence upon the prayers of fellow church members is a great privilege. "To remember each other in prayer" is vital to the spiritual strength of the church. There would be far less criticism of anyone in the church by any other member if this part of the covenant were observed more fully. We are not likely to criticize anyone for whom we are praying earnestly. The apostle Paul often requested the prayers of the brethren for himself. Every successful pastor depends much upon the prayers of his church members. Every successful leader in any organization or in any phase of the church work is conscious of a need for the prayers of all.

"To aid each other in sickness and distress" is an expression of loving and compassionate concern the members of the church ought to have for each other's well-being in body, mind, and soul, which includes visiting and caring for the sick, ministering to the needy, comforting the sorrowing, strengthening the weak, and praying for the wayward.

This mutual concern, expressed in a compassionate way, will lead one "to cultivate Christian sympathy in feeling and courtesy in speech." Such will promote a warmhearted fellowship in the church, along with striving "to be slow to take offense, but always ready for reconciliation, and mindful of the rules of our Saviour to secure it without delay." This will avoid contention and divisions within a church and will encourage peace and harmony.

Maintaining active and up-to-date church membership should be an accepted part of the responsibility of church membership. "We moreover engage that when we remove from this place we will, as soon as possible, unite with some other church, where we can carry out the spirit of this covenant and the principles of God's Word." If all of the time that is spent in trying to enlist non-resident members could be spent in witnessing to lost people, what a difference would be made in the number of converts, in additions to the churches by baptism each year, and in the real growth of the kingdom of God!

Perhaps many unenlisted Baptists should be approached as unsaved people. This might put them to shame and provoke the ones who are really saved to do something to convince others of their saving knowledge of Christ, through letting their lights shine for the glory of God. It might be most alarming if it could be known how many unenlisted church members are not in the kingdom of God.

" . . . by their fruits ye shall know them" (Matt. 7:20).

Eight

The Laws of the Kingdom

BEING SAVED by grace through faith makes one subject to the laws of the kingdom of God. The reference here is not to the ceremonial law and not to legalism, in the sense that some might think of keeping the moral law as a means unto salvation. The laws of God's kingdom are both moral and spiritual. They operate from within rather than by being superimposed. Any kingdom must have laws that are both forceful and fruitful if the kingdom is to be constructive and influential. Without law there is chaotic confusion.

The kingdom laws operate within the heart life of the kingdom subject. There is a vast difference between external commands and internal motivations. There is a big difference between outward compulsion and inward constraint. There is an obvious difference between coercion from without and conviction from within. There is a decided advantage in obedience to laws that are written on the heart as contrasted to laws that are written on tablets of stone or those that are found on the printed page. The apostle James writes about the "implanted word," as we have it in the American Standard Version of James 1:21. The suggestion of the seed planted in the heart sheds light upon the principle of God's laws being written upon the heart. God says, through his

103

prophet Jeremiah, "I will put my law in their inward parts, and write it in their hearts" (Jer. 31:33). With the law written in the heart, the subject of the kingdom becomes an incarnation and an exemplification of God's laws. Paul wrote to the Corinthians, "Ye are our epistle . . . known and read of all men" (2 Cor. 3:2). The greatest exponent of the laws of the kingdom is the one upon whose heart God's laws are indelibly inscribed. The greatest expositor of the laws of the kingdom is the man who exemplifies God's laws in daily living.

The "implanted word" is a sanctifying force in the heart life of the kingdom subject. God expects his kingdom laws to become a vital part of his kingdom people. What God told Ezekiel to do reminds us of how he must intend that his laws shall become an integral part of his children. To Ezekiel he said, "Eat this roll" (Ezek. 3:1). God wants his laws to be partaken of and assimilated into the moral and spiritual fibers of one's being. The Word of God informs, instructs, inspires, and nourishes the child of God. His Word functions to tell one what to do and then to give him strength with which to do it.

The law of God in the heart is an experience that is real, vital, and purposeful. There is delight in keeping the law of God when it is in the heart. Paul could say, "For I delight in the law of God after the inward man" (Rom. 7:22). This law in the heart is "not of the letter, but of the spirit" (2 Cor. 3:6).

This message from God is not only *to* his kingdom subjects, but it is also to be *through* his kingdom subjects—a message "known and read of all men" (2 Cor. 3:2). This is the message that the illiterate can read; it is the message that the farsighted and the nearsighted can read; it is the message that the idle and the busy can read. The law written in the heart takes precedence over externalism, legalism, formalism, and ceremonialism. The law in the heart eliminates the hirelings and the fearful with respect to obedience and performance.

The law in the heart produces service from the heart. Real fruitfulness is dependent upon the preparation and response of the heart. Jesus said in the parable of the soil, "But that on the good ground are they, which in an honest and good heart, having heard the word, keep it, and bring forth fruit with patience" (Luke 8:15). "A good man out of the good treasure of the heart bringeth forth good things" (Matt. 12:35).

Jesus condemned lip service when the heart was alienated from him. "This people . . . honoureth me with their lips; but their heart is far from me" (Matt. 15:8). In this he was referring to the pharisaical legalists of his day. The apostle Paul calls upon Christ's servants to do the will of God from the heart (Eph. 6:6).

The worship and praise of God should be from the heart— "singing and making melody in your heart to the Lord" (Eph. 5:19). David declared, "I will praise thee, O Lord, with my whole heart" (Psalm 9:1).

Genuine love for the Lord must be of the heart. Paul wrote to the Romans on this subject, "And hope maketh not ashamed; because the love of God is shed abroad in our hearts by the Holy Ghost which is given unto us" (Rom. 5:5). The apostle's prayerful interest in the Thessalonians was that "the Lord direct your hearts into the love of God" (2 Thess. 3:5). Jesus calls upon his followers, the subjects of the kingdom, to "love the Lord thy God with all thy heart" (Matt. 22:37).

From Mount Nebo in the long ago Moses appealed to the Israelites, saying, "Set your hearts unto all the words which I testify among you this day" (Deut. 32:46).

Laws must be authoritative to be effective. Christ is the authoritative lawgiver for the kingdom of God. The most complete discourse of Jesus is the Sermon on the Mount, which might well be entitled "The Laws of the Kingdom." At the conclusion of this discourse we read of the reaction of the people to his positive teachings: "And it came to pass, when Jesus had ended these sayings, the people were astonished at his doctrine: For he taught them as one having authority, and not as the scribes" (Matt. 7:28–29).

Christ is the supreme authority in the kingdom. He was aware of this authority when he said, "For the Father judgeth no man, but hath committed all judgment unto the Son" (John 5:22), and,

"All power is given unto me in heaven and in earth" (Matt. 28:18). John the Baptist declared, "He that cometh from heaven is above all" (John 3:31). The apostle Paul declared Christ to be "far above all principality, and power, and might, and dominion, and every name that is named, not only in this world, but also in that which is to come" (Eph. 1:21).

Christ, as the supreme authority in the kingdom, must be the one and only Master for the Christian. The Lord Jesus said to his kingdom subjects, "But be not ye called Rabbi: for one is your Master, even Christ; and all ye are brethren" (Matt. 23:8). Obedience to him as Lord is required. What a searching question it was when he asked, "And why call ye me, Lord, Lord, and do not the things which I say?" (Luke 6:46)! This may be a day of four-lane highways, twin motors, bifocal lens, bicameral systems of government, two-tone cars, twin beds, and dual wheels, but it must not be a day of two masters and dual lives.

Our Lord states the impossibility of serving two masters in the familiar words: "No man can serve two masters: for either he will hate the one, and love the other; or else he will hold to the one, and despise the other. Ye cannot serve God and mammon" (Matt. 6:24). The apostle Paul declares, "Ye cannot drink the cup of the Lord, and the cup of devils: ye cannot be partakers of the Lord's table, and of the table of devils" (1 Cor. 10:21). An attempt to serve two masters sets up an irreconcilable conflict in one's own life. It is the folly of striving to go in opposite directions at the same time.

Christ is worthy in his person, through his unique relationship to God the Father as the only Son of his kind. He has lived eternally with the Father as one who is coexistent with the Father and equal to the Father. He is the supreme revelation of God to man, ". . . being the brightness of his glory, and the express image of his person, and upholding all things by the word of his power" (Heb. 1:3). He is the sinless Son of God who, being without sin, could die for the sins of the world.

He has power over death, having overcome death, hell, and the grave. Through him "death is swallowed up in victory" (1

Cor. 15:54). He has "led captivity captive," and triumphantly reveals himself in a postresurrection appearance to be "alive forevermore." "I am he that liveth, and was dead; and, behold, I am alive for evermore, Amen; and have the keys of hell and of death" (Rev. 1:18).

He is worthy of our allegiance through the position that he now has at the right hand of God—as Sovereign Lord, Intercessor, Mediator, Saviour, and Judge. He is worthy of our obedience as Prophet, Priest, and King. "Worthy is the Lamb that was slain to receive power, and riches, and wisdom, and strength, and honour, and glory, and blessing. And every creature which is in heaven, and on the earth, and under the earth, and such as are in the sea, and all that are in them, heard I saying, Blessing, and honour, and glory, and power, be unto him that sitteth upon the throne, and unto the Lamb for ever and ever" (Rev. 5:12–13). What a climactic recognition of his worthiness!

One-master Christians are those who trust implicitly in Christ as Saviour and obey him as Lord. Their faith is not divided between Christ and the pope or priest. Their loyalty is not divided between Christ and the ordinances or ecclesiasticism. One-master Christians love the Lord supremely and take seriously his words, "If ye love me, keep my commandments" (John 14:15). Supreme loyalty to Christ calls for supreme loyalty to his kingdom. "Seek ye first the kingdom of God, and his righteousness" (Matt. 6:33) is the admonition of our Lord. The law of the kingdom is found in the priority of the kingdom.

In considering the laws of the kingdom, we do well to remember that Christ is not only our authority and sovereign Lord, but he is also our worthy example. The sure and safe way of distinguishing between right and wrong is to make the evaluation by the standard of Christ. Decisions concerning both words and deeds may well be made through asking and answering the questions, "What would Jesus say?" and "What would Jesus do?" Christ's standards surpass the law of Moses. Under the Mosaic law the sinful act was forbidden; under the law of Christ the sinful thought is forbidden. Under the Mosaic law sinful acts were condemned; under the law of Christ sinful attitudes are condemned.

Christ, as the standard of excellence, gave his own testimony of his obedient relationship to the Father when he said, "I do always those things that please him" (John 8:29). He is the example in the kingdom. "Because Christ also suffered for us, leaving us an example, that ye should follow his steps" (1 Peter 2:21). Christ holds up a high standard, for he says, "Be ye therefore perfect, even as your Father which is in heaven is perfect" (Matt. 5:48). The only hope of perfection is in God's perfect acceptance of us through the perfected merit of Jesus Christ, "Whom we preach, warning every man, and teaching every man in all wisdom; that we may present every man perfect in Christ Jesus" (Col. 1:28). In Christ is found consistency and an abiding sameness. A person does not have to be troubled about fluctuating standards, for "Jesus Christ [is] the same yesterday, and to day, and for ever" (Heb. 13:8).

The laws of his kingdom are unchangeable even as his word is unchangeable. In the governments of the state and nation laws are changing so rapidly that it is impossible for any one person to be acquainted with all the changes that are being made every time the legislative bodies convene, but God's word changes not. "For ever, O Lord, thy word is settled in heaven" (Psalm 119:89). Jesus declared, "Heaven and earth shall pass away, but my words shall not pass away" (Matt. 24:35). Peter quoted Isaiah, "The grass withereth, and the flower thereof falleth away, but the word of the Lord endureth for ever" (1 Peter 1:24-25).

The psalmist declared, "All his commandments are sure" (Psalm 111:7). God means what he says and says what he means. He is not a soft grandfather type who can be pushed around by the varied whims of his children. Concerning the certainty of God's law, Jesus said, "For verily I say unto you, Till heaven and earth pass, one jot or one tittle shall in no wise pass from the law, till all be fulfilled" (Matt. 5:18). The Lord speaks with finality, "For I am the Lord: I will speak, and the word that I shall speak shall come to pass" (Ezek. 12:25). There is no repeal of what God has decreed, and there is no appeal from his decree. "Ye shall not add unto the word . . . neither shall ye diminish ought from it, . . . ye may keep the commandments" (Deut. 4:2). Jesus said, ". . . the scripture cannot be broken" (John 10:35). Transgressors may break themselves against the laws of God, but in reality they never break his laws.

The ideal for the kingdom subjects is to be separate from the world. Concerning that intimate group of disciples, Jesus said in his intercessory prayer to the Father, "They are not of the world, even as I am not of the world" (John 17:14).

The spirit of Christ is called for in every area of the life of the kingdom subject—home life, business life, recreational life, as well as church and religious life. The spirit of Christ is the spirit of love, mercy, forgiveness, compassion, obedience, patience, perseverance, humility, and sacrifice. These Christian graces must characterize the kingdom subjects.

Jesus now reigns in spiritual Zion. Jesus is the rightful King to spiritual Israel but not to national Israel. Jesus was never anointed to be a national king. "My kingdom is not of this world" (John 18:36). "Behold, thy King cometh" (Matt. 21:5) may be applied to both Jews and Gentiles. The new covenant with the house of Israel and Judah referred to in Hebrews 8:8–9 must apply to spiritual Israel. In connection with this new covenant, the Lord promised to put the laws of the kingdom in their minds and heart. "I will put my laws into their mind, and write them in their hearts" (Heb. 8:10).

Some may be inclined to raise the problem of sin that is in the world today through the power of Satan. Our Lord claims no dominion over the realms of darkness and damnation. He claims no dominion over the unregenerated and the unrighteous, who refuse to turn to him for mercy, pardon, and salvation. His dominion is over all that pertains to the Spirit, and "the fruit of the Spirit is love, joy, peace, longsuffering, gentleness, goodness, faith, meekness, temperance: against such there is no law" (Gal. 5:22–23). Someday the King will destroy the works of the devil. "For this purpose the Son of God was manifested, that he might destroy the works of the devil" (1 John 3:8). "The prince of this world is judged" (John 16:11). Our King is a conquering King. Ultimately, the victory shall be complete in the destruction of the world of sin. "Now is the judgment of this world: now shall the prince of this world be cast out" (John 12:31).

The laws of the kingdom are commensurate with the nature of the King and the kingdom and are adequate for the needs of the subjects of the kingdom. The kingdom is spiritual, the laws are spiritual, and the subjects are spiritual, having been born of the Spirit of God. "For as many as are led by the Spirit of God, they are the sons of God" (Rom. 8:14). The subjects must worship God in spirit and in truth. "God is a Spirit: and they that worship him must worship him in spirit and in truth" (John 4:24).

The qualities of the kingdom are spiritual, being in the Holy Ghost: "For the kingdom of God is not meat and drink; but righteousness, and peace, and joy in the Holy Ghost" (Rom. 14:17). From this reference it may well be said that the laws of the kingdom are laws or principles of righteousness, peace, and joy in the Holy Ghost.

While the laws of the kingdom are spiritual in nature, they have social, moral, and ethical implications and applications that should vitally influence every area of the Christian's life and relationships.

The laws of the kingdom are eternal, just as the King and the kingdom are eternal and just as the subject of the kingdom is the recipient of life eternal. King Jesus has said, "Heaven and earth shall pass away, but my words shall not pass away" (Matt. 24:35).

While the kingdom of God is the kingdom of grace, the fact must be recognized that there are certain laws of the kingdom for disciplining the subjects of the kingdom. These laws are for the good of the subjects and for the glory of the King. The child of the kingdom is as a disciple of Jesus, in school to Jesus. He has the blessed privilege of learning at the Master's feet from the Master Teacher and from the kingdom Lawgiver.

Jesus calls for some discipline on the part of his followers when he says, "Take my yoke upon you, and learn of me" (Matt. 11:29).

We are privileged to learn from him his laws both by precept and example. We must be linked with him, associated with him, and accept the responsibilities of discipleship to be a good student and subject of the laws of the kingdom.

Some of the training may be quite rigid. Jesus never promised the kingdom subjects a flowery bed of ease. He called for stern discipline, involving self-sacrifice and self-denial, and promised his followers no exemption from persecution and other hostile treatment such as was meted out to him by his enemies. Jesus said, "It is enough for the disciple that he be as his master, and the servant as his lord" (Matt. 10:25). He wanted his kingdom subjects to know that one of the laws of the kingdom was the law of self-denial, but that it was not to be without its rewards. For he said, "He that loseth his life for my sake shall find it (Matt. 10:39).

One must recognize certain restraints that are imposed upon those who are blessed with the "glorious liberty of the children of God." The restraints are for the purpose of attaining unto, and experiencing, the larger freedom through deliverance from life's limitations that are often self-imposed. There is liberty in law, and there is bondage in lawlessness. The liberty of the Spirit comes to those who are willing to abide by spiritual laws and to those who are willing to "walk in the Spirit" (Gal. 5:16) and to "live in the Spirit" (Gal. 5:25). The liberty in Christ is not to be taken as an occasion to the flesh. No spiritual liberty is ever to be interpreted as a fleshly license.

Liberty of accurate performance comes only to the disciplined. One may think of the skilled musicians who perform with ease and efficiency only after years of rigid discipline in study and arduous practice. The liberty of the skilled surgeon is the blessing that has come after years of self-discipline. The greatest Christians are those who work at the business of being a Christian; they willingly surrender their lives to the King and willingly, cheerfully, and lovingly abide by the laws of the kingdom. The highest and most constructive forms of freedom are those that operate within law. The greatest slavery comes to those who incarcerate themselves through ignoring the laws of the kingdom of God and fall into their own snares.

In the kingdom of God liberty in law is paradoxical—we die to live, surrender to conquer, lose to find, abase to be exalted, hate the world in order to love God more fully, and dispossess ourselves in order more fully to possess the Lord. On the other hand, there are innumerable victims in the world who have lost their liberty by pursuing liberties without law. The all-wise God knows his kingdom subjects and has provided kingdom laws in line with needed restraints. Temptations are prevalent, and man's weaknesses are obvious; hence, there are many kingdom laws for man's self-protection and self-preservation.

Because of man's proneness to wander, God sometimes hedges him about with fences for his protection and guidance. We are as little children, in need of marked boundary lines for our lives lest we wander aimlessly and dangerously into the pitfalls of life. But God never fences us in a circle. His discipline is always to open the way to progress. The fenced lane of life may be but the path to the green pastures beyond and to the still waters.

The laws of the kingdom are designed to lead us into the larger meaning of salvation. The limited conception of salvation makes the religion of Christ a sort of a fire-escape religion and provides a bare entrance into heaven when this earthly life is over. The writer recalls the remark by an elderly lady, "I'll be satisfied if I just get inside the pearly gates." There is more to salvation than this narrow conception of it holds.

The laws of the kingdom emphasize the salvation that is *from* something *to* something and *for* something. Salvation is from sin's guilt, bondage, practice, penalty, and power. Ultimately, God's children shall be saved from sin's presence. Salvation is from death, darkness, despair, and damnation.

Salvation is to life that is abundant and eternal. Salvation is to righteousness, joy, and peace. The ethical implications of salvation must not be overlooked. The production, cultivation, and development of Christian character and conduct enter into the larger meaning of salvation in which the proper regard for the laws of the kingdom may play such a vital role. The writer of Hebrews said, "But, beloved, we are persuaded better things of you, and things that accompany salvation, though we thus speak" (Heb. 6:9). The child of the kingdom may well be expected to exemplify in character and conduct those qualities of life that are harmonious with, and worthy of, the Saviour and the great salvation. The pursuit of the kingdom subjects was called for by the apostle Paul when he wrote to Timothy, "Follow after righteousness, godliness, faith, love, patience, meekness" (1 Tim. 6:11). Paul also admonished Timothy to exercise himself unto godliness (1 Tim. 4:7). Children of the kingdom are to be servants of righteousness: "Being then made free from sin, ye became the servants of righteousness" (Rom. 6:18).

The larger meaning of salvation ultimately includes the heavenly home, which is the grand climax around the throne of King Jesus; but God is not pleased when our moral and spiritual lives are cramped and crowded by the things of the world until we fail to develop spiritually in line with the laws of the kingdom. The larger meaning of salvation cannot overlook the purposes of salvation. The saved are saved to serve. "For we are his workmanship, created in Christ Jesus unto good works, which God hath before ordained that we should walk in them" (Eph. 2:10).

The saved are also saved for fellowship with God the Father through Christ. "God is faithful, by whom ye were called unto the fellowship of his Son Jesus Christ our Lord" (1 Cor. 1:9). "Truly our fellowship is with the Father, and with his Son Jesus Christ" (1 John 1:3). The laws of the kingdom are designed to produce and to promote a greater fellowship between God and his children and among his children.

The laws of the kingdom are designed to show the kingdom subjects the importance of giving God the glory in our salvation —"That ye should shew forth the praises of him who hath called you out of darkness into his marvellous light" (1 Peter 2:9).

The laws of the kingdom of God are designed to produce growing Christians. Respect for the laws of the kingdom will produce strong Christians who are not satisfied to become stagnant and complacent. "Add to your faith virtue; and to virtue knowledge; and to knowledge temperance; and to temperance patience; and to patience godliness; and to godliness brotherly kindness; and to brotherly kindness charity" (2 Peter 1:5–7).

The laws of the kingdom call upon God's children to live as the sons of God. What a privilege it is to be children of God! "Behold, what manner of love the Father hath bestowed upon us, that we should be called the sons of God" (1 John 3:1). God's kingdom laws remind his subjects of their identity in their relationship to the King and of what may be expected of those who belong to God.

The laws of the kingdom that are designed for the discipline of the subjects of the kingdom, when enforced, may provide for the chastisement of God's children. Chastisement may prove the love of God for the one disciplined and may prove that the chastised belong to him. "For whom the Lord loveth he chasteneth, and scourgeth every son whom he receiveth. If ye endure chastening, God dealeth with you as with sons; for what son is he whom the father chasteneth not? But if ye be without chastisement, whereof all are partakers, then are ye bastards, and not sons" (Heb. 12:6–8).

Chastisement is for the good of the children of God. "Blessed is the man whom thou chastenest, O Lord, and teachest him out of thy law" (Psalm 94:12). "Now no chastening for the present seemeth to be joyous, but grievous: nevertheless afterward it yieldeth the peaceable fruit of righteousness unto them which are exercised thereby" (Heb. 12:11). "Behold, happy is the man whom God correcteth" (Job 5:17). The children of the kingdom must have the right attitude toward the enforcement of the laws of the kingdom through chastisement. "My son, despise not thou the chastening of the Lord, nor faint when thou art rebuked of him" (Heb. 12:5). Humble submissiveness should characterize the attitude of the kingdom subject toward chastisement. "Furthermore we have had fathers of our flesh which corrected us, and we gave them reverence: shall we not much rather be in subjection unto the Father of spirits, and live?" (Heb. 12:9).

The laws of the kingdom impose certain responsibilities upon the subjects of the kingdom. There are two important but simple words in the administration of the kingdom of God—"come" and "go." The invitation of our Lord is, "Come unto me" (Matt. 11:28). We come unto him for discipleship but go out from him for apostleship. Jesus said, "As my Father hath sent me, even so send I you" (John 20:21). "As ye go, preach" (Matt. 10:7). "Go ye into all of the world" (Mark 16:15). The law of the kingdom requires that the kingdom subjects shall be ambassadors of Christ. "Now then we are ambassadors for Christ, as though God did beseech you by us: we pray you in Christ's stead, be ye reconciled to God" (2 Cor. 5:20).

The royal law of the kingdom is the royal law of love. The law of love lifts our relationship to the King from one of required legalism to that of preferred grace. Love transforms coercion into choice. It transforms duty into privilege. Love yields to the exacted mile and gives the second mile. Love surrenders the coat and gives the cloak. Love not only forgives the offender but ministers to the offender. The royal law of love is the balance wheel of the religion of Christ, and without love one's religious experience may become quite unbalanced, aimless, and fruitless. Using the Revised Standard Version of the thirteenth chapter of First Corinthians, where the word "love" replaces "charity," we find that emotionalism without love is only so much meaningless noise. In the following quotation the King James Version is followed except where "love" is used instead of "charity":

"Though I speak with the tongues of men and of angels, and have not love, I am become as sounding brass, or a tinkling cymbal" (1 Cor. 13:1). Intellectualism without love amounts to nothing: "And though I have the gift of prophecy, and understand all mysteries, and all knowledge; . . . and have not love, I am nothing" (1 Cor. 13:2). Miraculous achievement without love is meaningless: ". . . and though I have all faith, so that I could remove mountains, and have not love, I am nothing" (1 Cor. 13:2). Humanitarianism without love profits nothing: "And though I bestow all my goods to feed the poor, . . . and have not love, it profiteth me nothing" (1 Cor. 13:3). Asceticism without love profiteth nothing: ". . . and though I give my body to be burned, and have not love, it profiteth me nothing" (1 Cor. 13:3).

Love is the basis for all blessed relationships in the kingdom of God. The royal law of the kingdom is that "we love him, because he first loved us" (1 John 4:19). Divine love has exercised the initiative to beget the children of the kingdom, and since love begets love, the chief objects of God's love respond with love. Love is the test of one's place in the kingdom: "He that loveth not knoweth not God; for God is love" (1 John 4:8). Love is the proof of one's place in the kingdom: "We know that we have passed from death unto life, because we love the brethren" (1 John 3:14). "Every one that loveth is born of God, and knoweth God" (1 John 4:7). Love is the highest motive for kingdom service: "For the love of Christ constraineth us" (2 Cor. 5:14).

When the royal law of love is properly functioning, the relationships between the subjects of the kingdom are acceptable to the King and a joyous fellowship prevails. God's people are bound together in spiritual unity by the cords of love. They accept and share mutual responsibilities in love and, in a co-operative way, propagate the message of love. The early Christians placed much emphasis on the fellowship of the believers in Christ, because in love they were bearing one another's burdens. The children of the kingdom may fervently sing, "Blest be the tie that binds our hearts in Christian love."

Where the law of love reigns, petty jealousies and enmities flee. Where the law of love is applied, bickerings and strivings vanish. Where love is real, there is no place for an unforgiving, vengeful spirit; but, rather, peace and harmony hold sway.

In a study of the laws of the kingdom some consideration should be given to the principles of God's judgment. His laws call for rewards for the good and penalties for the bad. The laws of his kingdom provide for degrees of rewards and punishment according to the proportions of the good and the bad. No final judgment is necessary to determine whether an individual is going to heaven or to hell. One's eternal destiny is determined by what that accountable person does with Jesus Christ, God's Son and man's Saviour. The rejection of Christ means eternal condemnation, and the acceptance of Christ through saving faith means eternal salvation.

One principle of God's judgment is that of truth. Paul declared, "But we are sure that the judgment of God is according to truth" (Rom. 2:2). Again, Paul said, "God shall judge the secrets of men by Jesus Christ according to my gospel" (Rom. 2:16). This statement may be related to the judgment according to truth, since Jesus declared himself to be the truth, "I am . . . the truth" (John 14:6); and since Jesus declared the word of God to be the truth, "Thy word is truth" (John 17:17).

Another principle in the laws of the kingdom for judgment is that judgment shall be according to deeds. The apostle Paul wrote these words to the Romans about God's judgment, "Who will render to every man according to his deeds" (Rom. 2:6). To the Corinthians Paul wrote, "For we must all appear before the judgment seat of Christ; that every one may receive the things done in his body, according to that he hath done, whether it be good or bad" (2 Cor. 5:10). Our Lord is capable of discerning between the good and the bad, and he has a record of the deeds of men. On the Isle of Patmos John had a vision of the judgment: "And I saw the dead, small and great, stand before God; and the books were opened: and another book was opened, which is the book of life: and the dead were judged out of those things which were written in the books, according to their works" (Rev. 20:12).

A third principle of judgment in the laws of the kingdom is that men shall be judged according to light. Jesus said: "And this is the condemnation, that light is come into the world, and men loved darkness rather than light, because their deeds were evil. For every one that doeth evil hateth the light, neither cometh to the light, lest his deeds should be reproved" (John 3:19–20). The principle of light and darkness is closely connected with the principle of knowledge and ignorance. Jesus taught: "And that servant, which knew his lord's will, and prepared not himself, neither did according to his will, shall be beaten with many stripes. But he that knew not, and did commit things worthy of stripes, shall be beaten with few stripes. For unto whomsoever much is given, of him shall be much required" (Luke 12:47–48).

The law of greatness in the kingdom is worthy of consideration. Standards of greatness in the kingdom are quite different from those in the kingdoms of this world. Jesus said, "Whosoever therefore shall humble himself as this little child, the same is greatest in the kingdom of heaven" (Matt. 18:4). This statement of Jesus seems to shed some light upon what is found in Matthew 11:11, where Jesus says, "Verily I say unto you, Among them that are born of women there hath not risen a greater than John the Baptist: notwithstanding he that is least in the kingdom of heaven is greater than he." This does not mean that John the Baptist was not in the kingdom but, rather, that any who are more childlike in humility than John would be greater than he. It is a lesson in the true standard of greatness, which is humility. True humility is an acceptable standard of greatness in the kingdom. Humble service becomes the measure of greatness, according to the laws of the kingdom. "But he that is greatest among you shall be your servant" (Matt. 23:11).

What shall be the attitude of the kingdom subject toward the laws of the kingdom? Submissiveness to the will of God is the answer. Jesus prayed: "Thy kingdom come. Thy will be done in earth, as it is in heaven" (Matt. 6:10). In the garden of Gethsemane Jesus prayed, ". . . not my will, but thine, be done" (Luke 22:42). David testified, "I delight to do thy will, O my God: yea, thy law is within my heart" (Psalm 40:8). The psalmist's prayer was, "Teach me to do thy will; for thou art my God" (Psalm 143:10).

Submissiveness to his will applies to voluntary service in answer to the call of God, as indicated in Isaiah's response when he said, "Here am I; send me" (Isa. 6:8).

Submissiveness to God's will is submissiveness to the laws of the kingdom. A challenge is found in these words of Jesus: "I seek not my own will, but the will of the Father which hath sent me" (John 5:30). Living in harmony with God's will is the way to live in harmony with the laws of the kingdom. "Not every one that saith unto me, Lord, Lord, shall enter into the kingdom of heaven; but he that doeth the will of my Father which is in heaven" (Matt. 7:21).